Simple Guide Books
How to Live with Your
Land Rover Discovery I & II
On a Budget

By Jason Martin

On Demand Instruction LLC

Preface

To begin with, I was a mechanic for fifteen years, not a writer, so please keep that in mind as you read this book. I apologize in advance for my lack of academic style. Secondly, this is a simple guide written for everyone, not just mechanics and engineers. I have tried to keep as much technical nomenclature out of this book as possible.

I wrote this book because I love my Land Rover and I believe they can be very reliable and last as long as anything else on the road. Even with their reputation of being unreliable, the fact is, 70% of all Land Rovers are still on the road today.

This book includes most of the common gremlins that plague these vehicles and offers some uncomplicated solutions, good maintenance practices, reasonable upgrades, and parts recommendations.

I based this book on a 2004 Land Rover Discovery II with the 4.6 V8 but most of the tips relate to any Discovery I or II. I did not include any tips or tricks for the diesel engine specifically, but every non engine related chapter in this book will apply to both the gasoline and diesel vehicles.

What's so Great About a Land Rover?

There is one of two reasons you purchased this book; either you own a Land Rover or you want one. The Discovery has one of the highest customer satisfaction ratings in the world along with some of the most complaints. It is comfortable and sexy and will all but climb a tree. But they cannot be called inexpensive to own, especially, if you or your mechanic is unfamiliar with its quirks. I have owned several cars, trucks, and SUVs over the years and after owning my Discovery, I will never own any other brand of vehicle.

I spent my first career in the auto industry as an automotive mechanic and service manager working on all makes and models. I had many customers who followed my word as gospel as well as followed me when I would change garages. If any one of my customers would have told me that they were thinking of purchasing a Land Rover, I would have done everything in my power to change their minds.

Why, you might ask? People who drive Land Rovers, Saabs, BMWs, Mercedes, Audis, modern Volkswagens, Jaguars, and pretty much anything made in Europe get big smiles from the people who work at their local auto repair shops.

European vehicles use more expensive and harder to find replacement parts and mechanic labor on these vehicles tends to be 20% higher than their American or Asian counterparts. To give you an example: the first brake job on a Toyota Camry typically costs less than $100.00. The first brake job on your Land Rover will usually cost $1000.00 or more.

Most European and British vehicles are designed to perform well and not just get you down the road. When your Land Rover wears out its brake pads, it also wears out its rotors, which are made from a softer cast iron that allows more grip thus, better braking. Compared to American or Asian vehicles, the European shock absorbers are more expensive, ignition wires are more expensive, and pretty much most every part of these vehicles is more expensive.

I have looked online at some of the reviews and forums for Land Rovers, in general and the consensus is, if you want to love your Land Rover, avoid the dealership for repairs. The majority of the negative reviews are from people who think the dealership is the only expert available for their vehicle. Dealerships do know the vehicles they sell very well and their parts prices are fair but they charge much more in labor than a local mechanic.

Just finding a good mechanic who is familiar with your vehicle will save you around 50% and you will typically be better cared for. Also, independent mechanics or shops will sometimes know more of the tips and trick I have in this book. The only time a dealership is necessary is when your mechanic can't figure out a problem or you still have a warranty.

If the Land Rover is such a hassle, why bother? Well, I have seen the underside of most vehicles on the road today and without getting into a bunch of technical jargon, I wouldn't change a thing on any Rover. Although a little quirky, Land Rovers are fantastic SUVs. Jeep has even changed their suspension system on their Wrangler to what Land Rover has used since the '70s. It has beam axles front and rear with a coil spring at each corner. This is far superior to leaf springs whether off road or on. If you do not have coil springs in the rear, you have the system which uses, expensive to replace, air bags but has the added benefit of adjustable ride height.

Even though they look tall and skinny, as though they might tip over, the Discovery IIs have been called the best handling SUVs in memory. Also, the Discovery II is one of the few vehicles of its era that utilizes a four channel anti lock brake/traction control system which greatly increases braking and traction. In fact it is the same one found in the H1 Hummer the U.S. military uses. Even its shock absorbers look like they belong on a school bus instead of a truck. These large shocks give more control, and handle abuse and heat better than their smaller counterparts. And most importantly, a full box ladder frame, one of the strongest, best engineered ones I have ever seen.

Have you ever seen a rusty Discovery? Nope. On top of that amazing frame is bolted an all-aluminum body. Aluminum saves a lot of weight over steel, will not corrode, and is easy to repair. Even with the lightweight aluminum body, a Discovery is so over-engineered and tough that it weighs in at 4600 pounds. That's about the same as a Chevy Suburban!

The British are famous for there interior design. The award winning interior on a Discovery is beautifully designed, comfortable, and quiet. The seats sit high and the window sills and dash are low so your sightlines are spectacular; you almost feel like you are on display in a fish bowl. The only other vehicles available with the same off-road capabilities would be the Jeep Wrangler or the Hummer H1. I challenge you to take a long trip in one without contemplating suicide.

Before I end this chapter, I feel it is necessary to mention purchase price. You can pick up most used European and British vehicles for a song after they get up to 75,000 miles and they are oftentimes in great shape too. My 2004 Discovery was $38,000 new and I purchased it in 2012 for only $7,300 with 90,000 miles and in near showroom condition.

In conclusion, you really get the best of all worlds with the Discovery.

Parts

If you reside in the US, finding parts for your Land Rover can be a challenge. Although this is not always the case, I have found some unusual parts at my local AutoZone, O'Reillly's or Advance stores. Local auto parts retailers are in a very competitive market and will usually have some of the best prices, so always check here first. All of the standard maintenance parts for Land Rovers can be purchased from most auto parts retailers.

For more specific parts and upgrades there are, thankfully, companies who specialize in Land Rover parts and accessories. So if you are in the market for a big off-road bumper, a spare tire relocation bracket and braided brake hoses, you will need to see the companies below.

US Parts:

Atlantic British
www.roverparts.com
Located in New York and has a huge selection of parts from all over the world. They have spectacular customer service and even some How To videos on their website. Atlantic British has also taken some of the guess work out of certain projects by creating packages that have all the necessary parts . Their head gasket sets are particularly impressive.
British Pacific is the West Coast sister company to Atlantic British in California and has all of the same great parts and service.

Rovers North
www.roversnorth.com
1800-403-7591
Located in Vermont and has a huge selection of parts. What makes them a bit unique is that they have a great selection of Land Rover Genuine parts, plus a big

selection of after market wheels, interior parts, off road equipment, and interior parts like wood trim pieces.

Lucky 8

www.lucky8llc.com

716-898-8153

One of my favorite places to shop. They are located in New York and sell replacement and aftermarket parts. Another plus are the You Tube videos to help get that new part installed. Their prices are very reasonable.

Toddco

store.toddcosuspensions.com

423-596-0392

Toddco Suspensions, Inc carries some products that I have never seen anywhere else. They have lift kits, skid plates, wheel spacers, kits to lower the gearing in transfer cases and the only 5.0 liter, 300 horsepower engine I have seen. They are located in Georgia (US).

British 4x4 Outfitters

www.british4x4outfitters.com

210-393-7778

British 4x4 Outfitters is located in Texas and sells new, used, and reconditioned parts. The also have a lot of impressive off road accessories and gear. What really sets them apart is some of the weird stuff they carry that you can't find elsewhere like brand new manual transmissions and reconditioned steering wheels. They have reasonable prices too.

Roverland Parts

www.roverlandparts.com

877-443-9246

Roverland Parts are professional Land Rover dismantlers and sell high quality used parts. This is a great place to go if you need that one little switch or broken part that you cannot find anywhere else. They literally have every factory part available. You will find good prices, rebuilt transmissions, and differentials.

Rocky Road Outfitters

www.rocky-road.com
888-801-7271 Orders
435-654-1149 Tech
Rocky Road Outfitters is located in Utah. They specialize in hard core off road products for many different makes and models but do have some very cool products for Land Rover. This is the place to find hood vents, great prices on Old Man Emu parts, very cool original roof racks, and rock sliders, and you can even get a snow plow.

Rovah Farm

www.rovahfarm.com
501-562-0337
Rovah Farm is in Arkansas and they sell all of those little new and used parts that no one thinks of until they need it. Individual seals, nuts and bolts, fan switches, and even rebuild kits. The best part; their prices will make you feel like you own a Chevy.

RTE

www.rte-fab.com
858-333-1391 Orders
704-635-7305 Tech
RTE makes legendary armor and suspension systems for Land Rovers. They are firm believers in pushing your Land Rover as far as it can go. The also produce the re-worked watts linkage for lifted Rovers.

The Dealership

The local dealership in your area will usually carry an extensive inventory for any Land Rover. Their prices are not extravagant like dealerships for other makes. The best part; they are local and you don't have to wait for the part to arrive, just go get it (usually).

Summit Racing Equipment

www.summitracing.com
1800-230-3030
I have used Summit Racing Equipment since I owned my first vehicle. They do not specialize in Land Rover parts

specifically but carry roughly 300 parts and performance upgrades for the Discovery. This is a great place for universal upgrades such as mufflers, oil coolers, and performance brake parts.

These companies will have almost everything you can think of for your Rover and I have used many with good success. I will also give suggestions throughout this book of who to use for each specific project or repair.

Parts from the UK:

Of course the original home of Land Rover will have an extensive network of parts and accessories. Most of these companies will also ship worldwide, have a currency converter built in to their websites and carry stuff that can be hard to find anywhere else.

MM 4X4

www.mm-4x4.com
01905-451506 Local
+44(0)1905-451506 International
MM4x4 is one of the largest independent Land Rover parts and accessories dealers in the UK. Here you can find tubular winch bumpers, light pods, 2" extended bolt-on wheel arches, and many other cool products. Warning! Wear sun glasses before looking at their website. It's bright yellow.

John Craddock

www.johncraddockltd.co.uk
01543-577207 Local
+44 (0) 1543-577207 International
John Craddock has been in business since 1970 and like many of us fell in love with his first Land Rover right away. Craddock carries everything from bulbs to bridging ladders and will happily work with international customers.

Paddock Spares and Accessories

www.paddockspares.com
08454-584499 Local
+44-1629-760877

Paddock Spares and Accessories carry a full line of parts, accessories and tools. They have an extensive website with tons of great gear. They have warehouse buying power which keeps their prices low.

Tools

General Tools

Any vehicle will require some specific tools, but a general set can still save a ton of money if you are willing to get a little dirty. Owning a Land Rover you will want to have both metric and SAE (inches) in both sockets and wrenches. Most full socket sets come with ¼, ⅜ and ½ drive ratchets, extensions and sockets, all are required. Land Rover also uses both 6 point and 12 point bolts so both kinds of sockets will be needed as well. A 12 point socket will fit on a 6 point bolt but will lack grip and may round the fastener. For example, the exhaust manifold bolts are ½ inch 12 point and head bolts are 15mm 6 point. Many metric and SAE sizes will interchange or work in a pinch but, it will be found that one or the other will fit better, such as the 5/16 or 8mm for the valve covers (the 5/16 fits tighter). Also, a large ½ inch drive breaker bar will come in handy, especially for head bolts or if rust is an issue. If the socket set chosen does not include deep sockets, you may want to purchase a set of these in ⅜ drive as well.

A home mechanic can get away with less expensive tools, such as those from Craftsman, where you still get a lifetime warranty and great quality. One should be able to get a whole set, with everything needed for less than $500.00. A professional mechanic will spend roughly $30,000 on a tool set from companies like Snap On and Mac, but these tools are designed to be used all day, every day and would be overkill for personal use on one vehicle.

Specialty Tools

A scan tool is a must for any tool kit today. Have you ever had a "Service Engine Soon" light come on? There is no way to find out what is happening without a scan tool. Even leaving a gas cap loose will trigger this light and the only option to turn it off, is to go to a parts store or service shop and have it scanned.

Thankfully, scan tools are not super expensive or difficult to use. Actron produces the model #CP9580A that will scan just about everything including the anti-lock brakes. This tool can be purchased at Summit Racing Equipment for about $200.00 and can be used on most other 1996 and newer vehicles as well.

If a laptop is handy, an Australian company called Total Car Diagnostics sells the TOAD software and an OBD cable that plugs into the USB port of any computer. All vehicles were standardized to use the OBDII (On Board Diagnostic) communications port in 1996. Prior to this, auto manufacturers all had different ways to talk to a vehicle's computer, which meant, a very expensive scan tool with a ton of adapters.

I personally use the TOAD software and found it to be better than any other hand held scan tool. The best part of this product is that a laptop has a much bigger screen for people with aging eyesight like me. The TOAD set up is also expandable to be used with pre OBDII systems and to tune almost any system in your vehicle. The kit with software and cable cost me a mere $100.00 and is very comprehensive.

To purchase the TOAD software and cable, go to:
www.totalcardiagnostics.com

Another special tool that is a must would be the torque wrench. A torque wrench measures the amount or twisting force being applied to a particular bolt. Each bolt and nut on a vehicle has a torque specification from the factory and proper torque is critical when reassembling a part of the vehicle. Too much torque and the bolt will break, too little and the part will leak or fall off.

Line wrenches are also a must for brake, power steering, and fuel lines. A line wrench is a semi-closed box end wrench that will help keep the line fittings from rounding, and believe me; they are usually difficult to loosen.

Miscellaneous Tools

Miscellaneous tools to consider are hammers, punches, oil filter wrenches, screw drivers, and pry bars. Many kits will include these, but just make sure you have them. A decent, heavy ball peen hammer can save hours of labor versus a small household hammer used to hang pictures. Also consider soft faced "no mar" hammers for when destroying a particularly stuck part is not in the plans.

Here is a list to make it easier:

- A set of metric box end wrenches from 8mm to at least 19mm
- A set of SAE box end wrenches from ¼ to 1 inch
- A set of line wrenches (most come as a kit with metric and SAE)
- A metric and SAE socket set with ¼, ⅜, and ½ drive ratchets and extensions. Both 6 point and 12 point sockets are preferred
- A set of ⅜ drive deep sockets in metric and SAE
- A ½ drive breaker bar
- A scan tool
- A ½ drive torque wrench
- A full screwdriver set and an interchangeable screwdriver with a large assortment of bits
- At least one medium pry bar
- A heavy ball peen hammer

- A soft face "no mar hammer" sometimes called a dead blow

Repair Manual

The best manual for Land Rover owners is the RAV Factory Manual. This is a free PDF download and is the most comprehensive repair manual available.

Download from: www.landroverresource.com

Air and Fuel

Air Delivery

An engine needs air to mix with fuel to make an internal combustion engine operate. There are a few options from the aftermarket to upgrade a Discovery, even turn it into a submarine. One of the more popular additions to Land Rover vehicles is a snorkel or raised air intake. Now don't take my submarine comment seriously, there are many more components that will die a horrible death when submerged, so do not throw a snorkel on your truck and drive it through a lake.

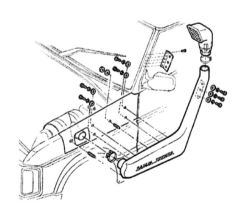

Basically this snorkel is a pipe that hooks directly into the stock air filter box with a water-tight seal. Not only does this look cool, but it is also very functional. Engines like cool air and a lot of it. Cooler air is denser and more oxygen rich, also cooler air generates more power, and sometimes more economy. The snorkel picks up air at roof level, away from road heat, dust, and water and will help the Discovery drive through water crossings, albeit with a few more modifications. The scary thing about installing a snorkel is cutting the body panels, although most come with great instructions. On this one, I would recommend using a body shop.

Caution! Here are the other modifications needed before making a water crossing:

First, the front and rear axles, transmission, and transfer case are all vented to allow for fluid expansion when hot. Without these vents fluid would push past the seals due to pressure build up. These are simple hoses that reach to the mid point of the vehicle. Atlantic British sells a vent extension kit just for this issue. Another task would be to make sure all of the electrical connectors are well sealed with silicon and the gas cap is well sealed. Finally make sure the weather stripping is in good shape as water entering the vehicle will destroy the computers that run the engine and transmission.

Atlantic British sells a drive train vent extension kit.
Most of the after market parts companies sell raised air intakes.

Many of these snorkels have a forward facing scoop which slightly raises the air pressure going into the engine. The vehicle will definitely get more air than the engine can use. With this set up, I would strongly recommend an oiled cotton gauze filter, such as the K&N, due to possible water or mud contamination. A paper filter will basically disintegrate when exposed to enough moisture and all of that material can then end up in the engine. Also the oil and gauze filter will typically last the life of the engine, is hand washable, and, allows almost no air restriction, even when filthy. The downside to these is slightly less filtration. Don't get me wrong, they will still do an adequate job but the stock style paper filter cleans the air better, allowing almost nothing through.

Most local auto parts stores sell both K&N and stock style air filters.

The air box that came from Land Rover is a very good design; it is water tight, has good flow characteristics, and can hold a significant amount of dirt or water below the filter level. The only problem is that they are made of cheap plastic and tend to break easily when changing your air filter.

When I purchased my vehicle it had a broken air box. This left me with two options:
1. Buy a new air box at a price of $300.00 or
2. Replace the whole assembly with something else.

Specter Clamp on Air Filter

Needless to say, being a cheapskate, I went with option 2. What I did was, purchase a clamp on, conical oil and gauze filter made by Specter for $25.00 from my local AutoZone. This simply allowed me to remove the old and broken air box and clamp the filter directly to the Mass Air Flow sensor. The plus point to this was a small boost in power and responsiveness the downside is, no snorkel, which is not a big deal because I didn't plan on installing one. The other downside is that the engine is now sucking in a bunch of under hood heat through the intake, but that downside hasn't seemed to affect anything adversely to date.

Clamp-on conical air filters can be purchased from most local auto parts stores or Summit Racing Equipment.

Mass Air Flow Sensor

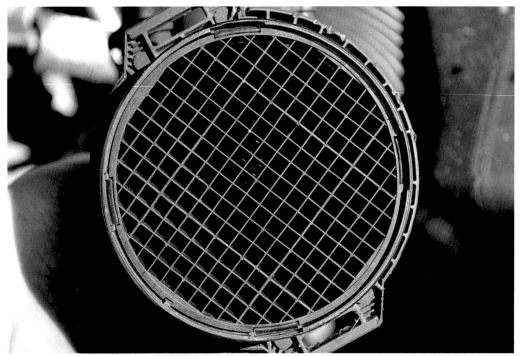

Mass Airflow Sensor

Modern Land Rover engines use a Mass Air Flow or MAF sensor to measure the amount of air coming into the engine and then feeds this data to the computer. The way this works is quite simple actually.

The mass air flow sensor is a tube that the incoming air passes through, after it is filtered and, before it gets to your manifold. This tube has a thin heated wire that runs through it, and the computer measures the amount of electricity it takes to keep that wire at a certain temperature. It then uses this information to adjust the amount of fuel to feed the engine. Even though the air moving through this sensor is filtered, it will get gummed up and will not send a correct signal.

The solution is to keep this sensor clean. I used to use brake cleaner to spray down this wire, which works well, but now you can go to your local auto parts store and purchase a chemical designed specifically for this task. I have seen 2MPG and a bit more power just from doing this and I recommend it at every oil change. It is something many mechanics either don't do or don't know about but it is essential to keep up efficiency and drivability.

CRC MAF Cleaner

Purchase CRC Mass Air Flow Sensor cleaner from most auto parts stores.

Fuel System Cleaners

On any vehicle I recommend using a fuel system cleaner every other oil change. Most of these cleaners are simply added to the fuel tank at fill up and will clean intake valves, injectors, and combustion chambers. Most quality gasoline will contain detergents that keep an engine pretty clean but the crankcase ventilation system will pull oil vapor and contaminants in to the combustion chamber as well, causing most of the carbon build up.

One of the best fuel system cleaners on the market is 44K made by BG Products Inc. The drawback to this is it also will wash the cylinder liners, causing more grip with the piston and sometimes cause the dreaded liner slipping known in the 4.6 Liter. A workable solution is to use the recommended amount of Marvel Mystery Oil in the next tank of fuel. This will help to lubricate the upper cylinders and rings again, stopping that loud ticking sound. I have torn down many engines and have recently had to dismantle an engine before and after using BG 44k. I can say that the BG product does do its job well.

More on Marvel Mystery Oil. I am not one to fall for magic pills and snake oil, but this stuff works wonders. The cleanest engines I have ever had the pleasure to dismantle used Marvel Mystery Oil in the gas at every fill up. I swear, these engines were actually as bright and shiny as new, after 100,000 miles. It does have to be used at every fill up to work as designed and can be purchased almost anywhere that sells automotive products. It works by coating everything with thin oil that simply disallows deposits to stick; it will also lubricate the fuel pump and injectors. Plus it is very inexpensive.

You might be asking yourself why the above mentioned engines needed to be dismantled if so clean. Simply, my customers neglected to change their timing belt on time, which smashed the pistons into the valves. (Don't worry, Rover V8s use timing chains)

What about the rest of the intake system? Well, every 30,000 miles, I also recommend cleaning the rest as well. There is a simple device anyone can make after a trip to the hardware store. All that is needed is about three feet of vinyl hose in 3/8, a couple hose barbs and, a valve.

Plug one end in to the PVC vacuum port on the intake plenum then put the other end into the bottle of cleaner.

I recommend using Sea Foam Motor Treatment or Marvel Mystery Oil. Sea Foam is actually designed to be used this way. Sea Foam also makes a pressurized version with a long straw that would negate your trip to the hardware store.

With the engine started, slowly turn the valve open just until the engine begins to run roughly. Continue at this rate until the bottle of cleaner is empty. Allow the engine to idle for an additional ten minutes before shutting down. Reconnect the brake booster line then take it for a drive.

Caution! There is a good possibility that you now have a Batman smoke screen installed on your vehicle. Any of the excess cleaner in the system or exhaust will start to burn off and will smoke like mad.

This process will clean the whole intake system, intake side head ports, intake valves and combustion chambers and is well worth the hassle.

Marvel Mystery Oil and Sea Foam can be found at almost any auto parts store

Brake System and Traction Control

Brake Replacement

You are in luck in this department. European manufacturers usually over engineer their braking systems with large soft rotors, multi piston calipers and large pads. The upside of this is tons of lock up-free stopping power. The downside to this is your rotors are not able to be machined and have to be replaced with every brake job. This project will usually run about $70.00 for each rotor.

A ton of money can be saved by just popping a new set of pads on your old rotors without machining. Just make sure your old rotors have enough thickness remaining. Most if not all rotors have a discard thickness and may risk over heating or warping, if not replaced when they reach this point. If you notice a pulsation when braking (very rare in Land Rovers) then replace the rotors because they are warped. A pulsation will typically manifest itself as a steering wheel shimmy while braking at highway speeds, think of your rotor looking like a vinyl record that you left in the sun (if anyone remembers vinyl records anymore.) Occasionally, if your rotors are fairly new, they will be able to be machined to solve the pulsation problem. Just check with your mechanic.

If re-using the old rotors, another thing to be careful of, is that it will take a lot longer to break in your new pads, usually 200 to 300 miles of normal driving. During the break in period give yourself a bit of extra stopping distance because the new pads will not have full contact yet.

Just remember that you can only do this once. After running two sets of pads on your one rotor, your rotors will be too thin. Thin rotors will run much hotter than normal and could cause the brake fluid to boil and brakes to fail.

My recommendations for standard or performance replacement brake parts are by a company called EBC. For standard replacement, I strongly prefer the EBC Ultimax pads and stock replacement rotors. These are the highest quality parts and will improve brake feel and grip. These pads and rotors are roughly 50% more expensive compared to cheap auto parts store replacements, but well worth it.

EBC Brake Pad

If a further upgrade is desired, EBC also has their Green Stuff pads or if you want to go nuts you can use the Yellow Stuff pads. These Green Stuff pads are a nice upgrade because they are softer and softer grips harder but softer also wears out faster and create a lot of dust. The upside to this softness is less rotor wear and roughly 20% better stopping power.

The Yellow Stuff pads are slightly different. They are made of a high friction formula and can handle a ton of heat and will last about as long as OE. The downside is they are fairly expensive and make as much dust as OE. The big upside is the 30-40% better braking, great for larger tires and towing.

Brake Rotor Upgrade

A popular brake upgrade many have adopted is the slotted, cross drilled or dimpled rotor. These were originally designed for racing back when brake pads were made of asbestos. When asbestos pads would heat up on the race track, they would off-gas. This gas would actually create a barrier between the pad and rotor which make the brakes not work well (if at all). These upgraded rotors effectively allowed this gas to escape or be scraped off of the pads, restoring braking power.

Today, asbestos is illegal to use in brake material in most places, and modern pads will rarely off gas. Also, all but teenagers who have watched the *Fast and the Furious* a hundred times would never get their bakes up to off-gassing temperature anyway. So this kind of negates the use of these more expensive rotors, plus the cross drilled rotors tend to crack between the holes.

However, there is a benefit to slotted or dimpled rotors. They will clean away dirt and water from your pads while you are off road or in the rain and allow some additional cooling while towing. Although most of us will never require the use of rotor upgrades such as these, they do look cool. Again, go with EBC brand for this upgrade especially when using their Green or Yellow Stuff brake pads, they are designed to work together.

EBC Pads and Rotors can be found at Summit Racing Equipment

Brake Hoses

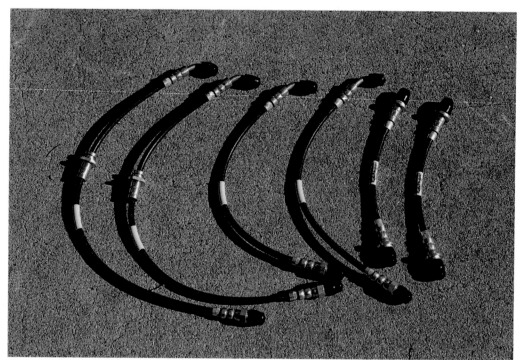

Stainless Steel Braided Brake Lines

Another nice upgrade is to replace your rubber brake hoses with stainless steel braided lines. First of all your rubber lines are probably already cracked and ready to be replaced. Secondly, every time you hit your brakes your hoses will swell slightly, causing some ambiguity in brake feel. Braided hoses won't swell and also don't wear out for a very long time. This is probably the least expensive way to greatly increase the effectiveness of the braking system.

Another benefit to these upgraded hoses is the extra control they will allow over the brakes. I strongly recommend this upgrade especially if a lift kit is involved and larger tires are used. Most companies will manufacture both stock and 2 inch longer versions. Longer brake hoses are rarely installed on most lifted vehicles and when the suspension drops to its full extent, stock brake hoses will snap, leaving the driver with no brakes.

Stainless steel brake lines can be purchased from Atlantic British

Brake Fluid

Brake fluid is one of the most neglected fluids in a vehicle's maintenance cycle. Brake fluid should be changed every 30,000 miles or two years. Brake fluid is hydroscopic which means it absorbs water to keep its hydraulic abilities. This is great but, water boils and so will the brake fluid when it gets hot. When someone says they lost their brakes while towing, this is usually the cause. This water will also start to corrode the cast iron parts in the brake system.

One way to achieve this bit of maintenance is to take it to your mechanic and get a brake system flush for usually less than $50.00.

Another way is to do it yourself:
1. Remove and replace all of the fluid from the master cylinder reservoir. Make sure the new brake fluid is coming out of a sealed container!
2. Get a buddy to help bleed all four of your brakes until all of the fluid looks new. Start at the wheel furthest from the master cylinder.

Keeping the fluid clean will also keep all of the hydraulic components in good working order which will save time and money in the long run.

Use a good quality DOT 4 or DOT 5.1 brake fluid from a sealed container. Do not use DOT 5 brake fluid as this will not hold up to daily use as it is hydrophobic and will create water pockets.

DO NOT use any other product in a brake system! I made a small fortune replacing whole brake systems because a customer put power steering fluid, transmission fluid, or motor oil in their master cylinder. Petroleum products will cause all of the rubber seals and hoses to swell and deteriorate, which eventually causes the brake pedal to go to the floor!

The Three Amigos

Imagine driving down the road, minding one's own business, then hearing a loud dinging noise and seeing three warning lights come on all at once. Unfortunately, most Discovery owners are familiar with this. The Three Amigos is nothing short of frightening to some people, I have even had customers pull over to the side of the road and have had their vehicle towed to me out of fear that it was no longer safe to drive.

What are they? What do they want?

It is pretty simple, really. These lights are for the anti-lock braking system, traction control, and hill decent systems. Still sounds scary? Interestingly, it is all the same system—not a catastrophic failure.

Anti-Lock Brakes

Here is a breakdown of how this system works. First, there is a sensor at each wheel that measures wheel speed. The computer monitors the speed of each wheel in relation to each other wheel. When braking, if a wheel stops moving (i.e., on ice, sand, etc.), it modulates that wheel to maximize braking traction and makes a farting noise that the driver can feel in the brake pedal. This is the antilock braking engaging.

Traction Control

When trying to accelerate on a slick surface, if a wheel starts to spin faster than another, the system modulates that brake which forces the power to the wheel or wheels with more traction—again making a very distinct farting sound. This is the traction control engaging and goes a long way to keep the Rover from getting stuck.

Hill Descent

Finally, there is a button inside the Discovery that shows an avatar of a Land Rover traveling down a steep incline; push this and it engages the hill descent. This allows the driver to navigate steep hills safely while off-road. For Land Rovers that never go off-road, they will never need to use the hill decent. What it does is apply the antilock brakes, finding the best traction for each wheel to keep the vehicle in control. You Tube is full of videos of 4x4s trying to go down a steep incline and then flipping end over end because the drivers hit their brakes too hard to slow down properly or ended up sliding sideways to the same effect.

So basically a Land Rover has four sensors, a modulator and a computer that run all three of these systems. Not really a whole lot to go wrong. Honestly, a Land Rover owner can drive the vehicle for the rest of its usable life and never fix this problem. It would be like having a vehicle without ABS, traction control, or hill decent except for the annoying warning lights.

The typical problem that brings the three amigos to the party is simply a faulty ground. Usually what happens when taking the Land Rover to the shop, to handle these amigos is; the mechanic reads the codes being displayed by the computer which are usually:

- SVS Long Term Supervision Failure
- One sticking SVS
- SVS Electrical Supervision Failure

Then he says to himself, "this guy has a bad ABS Modulator!" Then he says to the Land Rover owner, "You need a new ABS Modulator and a brake flush and it will cost you your first born child".

This is usually when people start to hate their Land Rovers, especially due to the fact that the three amigos are going to come back soon, because the problem isn't really fixed. The replacement modulator is built exactly the same as the one being replaced.

Thankfully the solution is a fairly simple one and it is cheap and permanent too. Here is the procedure:

ABS Modulator

1. Make some room to work. Remove the air box and intake pipe. Also, pull up the power steering reservoir and set it down where the air box once was. Loosen the four brake lines, with line wrenches, at the top of the modulator and the two on the side.

DO NOT use a box wrench as it can round off the nuts! Line wrenches are made specifically for brake and fuel lines, a 13mm and an 11mm are required. If you do not have line wrenches, get some!

DO NOT use any kind of lubrication! Most lubricants are petroleum based and will contaminate the brake system, causing damage to all rubber parts, thus turning this cheap fix into a very expensive one. Removing the modulator is recommended for this job, even though it is possible to complete without taking off the brake lines. Don't fret; it is not that hard to bleed the system when finished.

2. With everything out of the way, remove the three shock-absorbing mounts at the front and rear of the modulator that attaches the unit to the vehicle.

3. Remove the three electrical connections from the modulator. There are two in the front and one on the side of the unit. This picture also shows the rear mount. The front mount is just below the harness   connection indicated in this photo.

4. At this point the modulator can be propped up to get at the shuttle valve assembly, where the modification is made. This is fairly difficult as there is barely enough room to reach the screws with the wrench and the screws are thread locked.

Remove the modulator by first placing a shop towel under the unit to catch the brake fluid that will be released. Brake fluid is wonderful paint stripper but can be washed away with water, so have some handy. Now, remove the brake lines you loosened in step 1 and pull out the modulator.

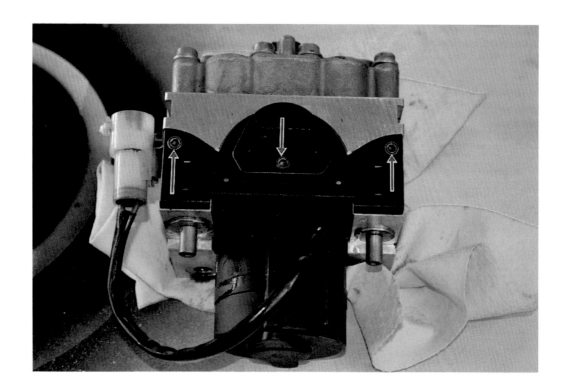

5. Place the modulator on a workspace with a rag under it to catch brake fluid. Remove the three, 4mm hex screws holding the shuttle valve cover in place. These have a thread sealer like Loctite applied at the factory so they will be hard to break loose (another reason to remove the whole unit.)

6. Pull up the cover enough to get to the two prong connector inside and disconnect.

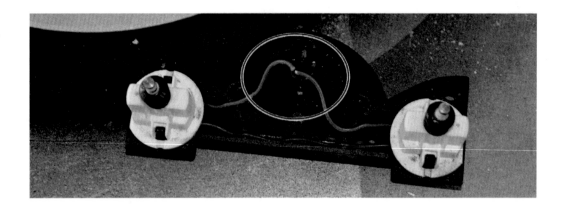

7. With the shuttle valves out, cut the connector from the two wires coming from the shuttle valves.

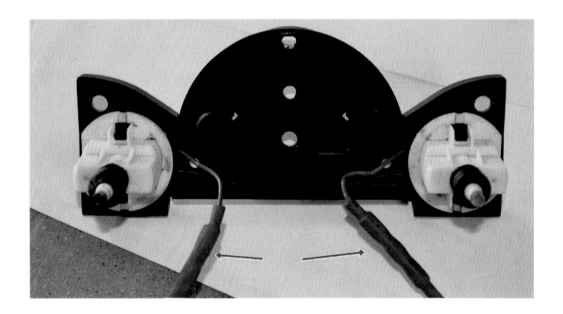

8. Use electrical butt connectors or solder to connect two 24" long 16ga, insulated wires to the existing wires. I strongly recommend using heat shrink tubing to cover the new connections. If this is unavailable, then electrician's tape will suffice. Just do your best to keep the connections water tight.

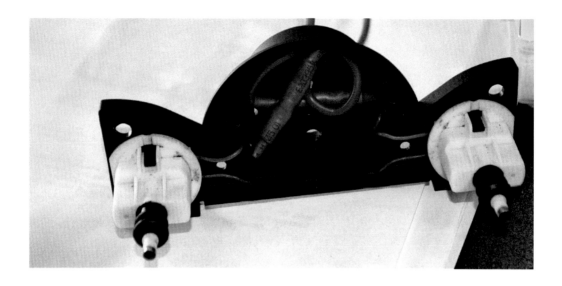

9. It may be required to enlarge to two existing holes where the connector was once held. Pull the new wires through the holes and tuck the connections into the shuttle valve cover.

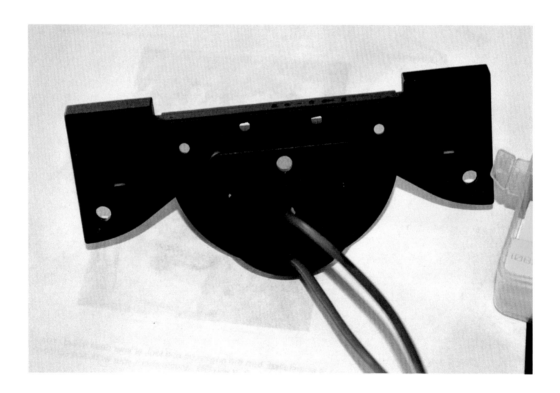

10. It should look something like this.

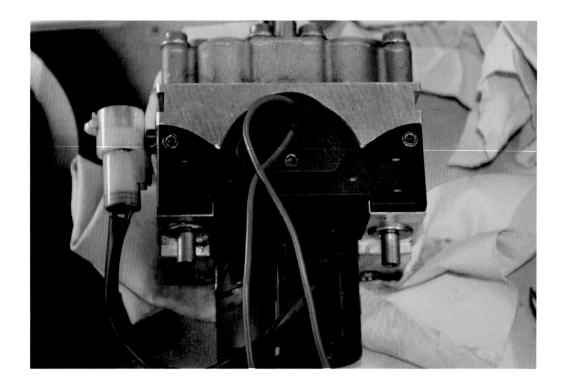

11. Apply a new coating of Loctite to the hex screws and reinstall the shuttle valve cover.

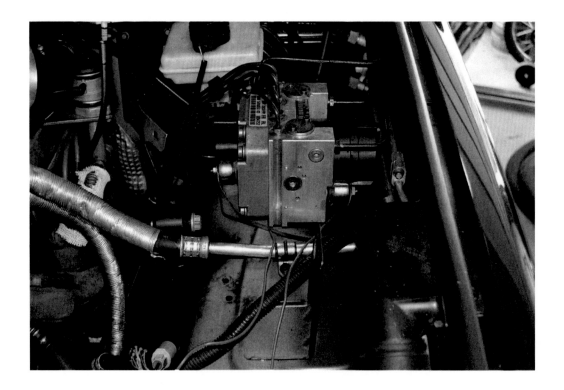

12. Reinstall the modulator. Tighten the mounts and then finger tighten the brake lines.

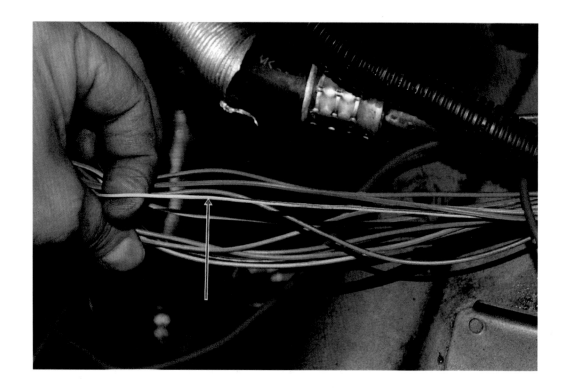

13. Pull the wires from the modulator's main wiring harness loom (plugs in to the front of the modulator). Locate the yellow/green wire and cut it.

14. Trim and attach either of the new wires, it does not matter which, to the end of the yellow/green wire going into the main harness, not the one going back to the modulator.

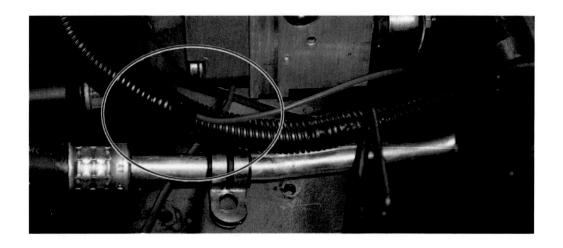

15. The other end of the yellow/green wire is now non functional and can be tucked inside the wire loom along with the other wires.

Use electrician's tape to secure the loom closed where the new wire exits the harness. The other new wire now needs to be grounded. A perfect spot is the hold-down bracket for the A/C line that runs nearby the modulator.

16. To make the ground as strong as possible, sand away some of the paint where the bolt attaches the bracket.

18. Trim new wire and attach a circle style connector. Reattach the bracket with the connector underneath, against the body of the vehicle.

19. Bleed the brake system:

DO NOT allow the brake fluid in the reservoir to fall below the (min) line while bleeding the system. Use only DOT 4 or DOT 5.1 brake fluid from a sealed container. Again, have a rag under the modulator to catch the fluid.

A second person will be required for this procedure to operate the brake pedal.

Start at the modulator. Have the second person depress and hold the brake pedal. **DO NOT PUMP THE BRAKES!** The six lines attached to the modulator should still be only finger tight and fluid/air should come from these connections. While the brake pedal is still being depressed tighten these six lines. **DO NOT** allow the brake pedal to be released before the lines are tight, air will be drawn back into the system.

With the lines tight, release the brake pedal and check the fluid level in the reservoir. Depress the brake pedal and hold it again. While the pedal is depressed, loosen one of the side brake lines on the modulator until fluid/air is released. When the fluid/air stops coming out then tighten the brake line. With the brake line tight, release the brake pedal.

Repeat step (4) for the other side brake line on the modulator, then again for each of the four lines on the top of the unit. Keep constant vigilance on the level of the brake fluid through out this procedure.

Once all six lines have been bled the first time through, go back and bleed all six again. Continue repeating this procedure until no more air is released. At this point, a nice firm pedal should be felt.

Some air may have moved down the lines if the pedal is not firm. If this is the case, a standard brake bleeding may be required at each wheel. Either, follow the procedure in the Rave Manual or perform step number (4) starting at the wheel closest to your driver's seat and moving to the next farthest wheel until all four are without air. Each of the brake calipers has a small nipple attached close to its top; this is the bleeder valve that will need to be loosened to allow the fluid/air to be released. Bleed each caliper several times to ensure no air remains.

That is it, no more Three Amigos! I performed this procedure on my Discovery four years ago and still have never had them return. Also my ABS, Traction Control, and Hill Decent all work flawlessly.

Chassis and Suspension

Up to 2004, Land Rover used the best all-around suspension system for almost all off road situations. For the 2005 models, the LR3 or Discovery III, Land Rover switched to four wheel independent suspension. Independent suspension does have benefits, mostly a comfortable ride and better handling.

The benefit of two coil sprung straight axles is strength and traction. Straight axles allow a vehicle to hold an alignment under heavy abuse and also handle that abuse without breaking. I once saw a guy hit a stump at 30mph with his Ford F350. It tore the front axle, suspension and steering components all the way back to the middle of the truck. The only thing salvageable was the front axle which was nearly undamaged aside from some missing paint.

Bowler, the famous off road racing truck builder, won tons of races and wowed the world with his straight axle Tomcats and Wildcats that were built on Land Rover platforms. So sure, we know they will work great for off road racing and are though; but they will also work better for trail runs and rock crawling? In these situations they are unbeatable.

The reason for this is when one wheel gets pushed up, going over a large rock etc., the wheel on the other side of the axle gets pushed down, which of course gives more traction. This also gives more suspension travel and articulation. Plus, when off road the wheels will continue to stay in a straight up and down camber, giving you more control. The drawback is less ride quality versus independent suspension. A straight axle vehicle, even one with coil springs built by Land Rover, is nothing short of bouncy.

Coil Springs vs. Leaf Springs

Coil springs have the benefit of more suspension travel, better ride and a more precise spring rate. They are also more durable. Leaf springs tend to break when put through stressful situations especially when modified. A leaf spring's weak point is right at the shackle eye and unless you carry around a portable welding rig, you are walking out when you are off-road. The only bad thing about a coil spring is it will typically dislocate (come out of its top mount) when your wheel drops too far. Not a big deal and it will usually pop itself back in, albeit with a scary sound; if it doesn't, it is fairly easy to re-install with a jack. Typically, this won't happen, unless you disconnect your sway bars and have longer shocks for more articulation and suspension travel, which can be really handy on a hard trail.

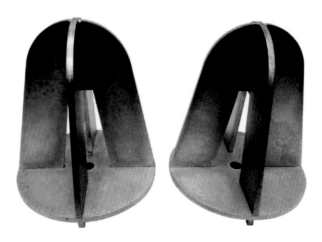

Terrafirma Dislocation Cones

If your Suspension has been modified; Terrafirma makes spring relocation kits for the front and rear of a Discovery. These simply guide the spring back into its perch.

Terrafirma Relocation Cones can be purchased from almost any Land Rover Specific parts company

Steering Rods

I have said it before, Land Rover has the toughest chassis and suspension I have ever seen on a production vehicle. It does although have a weak point which is the steering rods.

The stock steering rods on the Land Rover are made of super flimsy 0.80 tubing with a .10 wall thickness. This is sufficient for normal on and off road use. But if serious four wheeling is your thing, the steering rods may come into contact with a rock or stump, causing the linkage to bend. Once these rods bend, they will most likely have to be replaced to get the vehicle back in alignment. Switching to large tires and a suspension lift will sometimes allow for a big pothole to tweak these stock steering rods.

Many companies manufacture a much heavier duty steering rod kit made with much thicker materials for greater durability. Rovers North has a good selection and price on these. Most after market heavy duty rods are made from solid 30mm hardened steel.

Another good solution is to install a front skid plate. Skid plates can be purchased from most companies, will protect the steering linkages from anything, and add some cool off road style to boot. If working with a lifted vehicle and are running large tires, consider doing both.

Get either or both the Upgraded Steering Rods or the Skid Plates from most Land Rover specific parts stores

Power Steering System

The power steering system is very well thought out on Land Rovers and even has a fluid cooler. One big mistake some people make is to use automatic transmission fluid or cheap aftermarket power steering fluid instead of the recommended fluid. This will cause the power steering pump to leak in very short order or work poorly in temperature extremes. Any power steering pump will eventually fail but there is no reason to shorten its life, especially at a price of $400.00 for a replacement. The best fluid to use is the factory Land Rover power steering fluid or a synthetic type. The best, in my opinion, is Pentosin CHF 11s. If neither the factory nor the Pentosin brand is available, use what can be found at the auto parts store, as long as it is synthetic. Land Rover pumps are fairly sensitive and will complain if a non synthetic fluid is used, especially in cold weather. If you use a non synthetic fluid, make sure to replace all of the fluid in the system every 30,000 miles as a normal maintenance procedure. Pentosin claims to last forever, but I would change it every 100,000 miles to be safe.

Most standard auto parts stores either have Pentosin CHF 11s or can get it. Sometimes they keep it in the back due to its price. So if you don't see it on the shelf ask a sales person.

If the power steering pump does fail, thankfully, there is a rebuild kit. Kotek makes the rebuild kit SK-9170, unfortunately it is hard to find, but only about $25.00. I would recommend contacting the company at:

KOTEK AMERICA, INC.
17752 COWAN ST
IRVINE, CA 92614
TEL: 1.949.863.3126
FAX: 1.949.752.7706
TOLL FREE TEL: 1.888.865.6835
TOLL FREE FAX: 1.888.665.6835
E-MAIL: sales@kotek.com
Also, Ebay is sometimes a great place to find this rebuild kit.

Rebuilding the power steering pump is not all that scary and saves an incredible amount of money. There are also a few videos on You Tube that will walk anyone through the process.

The toughest part of the rebuild or replacement of any power steering component is getting the air out of the system. Land Rover installed a bleeder valve on the top of the steering box just for this purpose. Unfortunately, following the standard directions for bleeding the system will cover you and your vehicle and your assistant and your garage in power steering fluid. Doing a standard bleeding on the power steering system will also use about a gallon of fluid before all the air is out. This can be a very expensive endeavor with a high quality power steering fluid. A simple solution is to make feedback hose that returns all of the fluid back in to the reservoir while getting rid of the air. It looks like this:

All I did was use a 3/8 inch piece of clear vinyl hose, about 24 inches long with a hook made of 1/4 inch copper tubing at the end.

Simply hook the copper end in to the reservoir and attach the tube to the open bleeder nipple. Now, just turn the steering wheel lock to lock until all of the air is gone. **DO NOT** put a kink in the copper tubing when you bend it. This will cause the vinyl line to blow off the steering box making a big mess.

Shock Absorbers

Shock absorbers are constantly in motion as the vehicle is in motion. Like any moving part, they will eventually wear out. Most stock shocks have had it by about 50,000 miles. On a Land Rover, with mostly street use, one may see 80,000 to 100,000 miles out of their stock shocks. By 100,000 miles even the best shocks are fairly worn out and need to be replaced.

There are a few ways to figure out if your shocks have gone bad. The first is ride. With bad shocks the suspension will feel gushy over bumps and continue to bounce more than once after hitting the obstacle. Drivers may also experience their vehicle bottoming out. This is when the suspension hits its maximum compression over a bump; it feels like a sudden stop in motion. This may be a good indicator in most vehicles, but Land Rovers have a massive amount of upward suspension travel and would almost need to be jumped to make this test work.

Since ride quality diminishes gradually many people never notice that their vehicle rides like an old Viking ship, rocking back and fourth going down the road. Another way to see if shocks are bad is to check for leaking between the two halves of the shock, the thin oil is the consistency of WD-40. Tire wear is also a good indicator of worn shocks and they will look choppy across the width of the tread. By far the easiest way, is to go by mileage. Most shocks should be replaced at 50,000 to 60,000 miles and the top end shocks at 100,000.

Shock absorbers are more important than many people think. Most of my customers believed that shocks and struts only affect ride quality. In truth, bad shocks can greatly increase stopping distances, wear on all of the other suspension parts and previously mentioned tires.

Shocks come in many brands, colors, styles, and reputations. Most of the shock companies use a twin tube nitrogen gas charged or hydraulic design. Twin tubes have the advantage of extra protection from damage while in the rough, and they tend to be less expensive.

The downside to this design, compared to a premium mono tube shock is: less responsive driving, less ride quality, less road feel and less precise handling. Don't get me wrong, twin tube shocks will work fine, are very rugged, and will give you an average service life. Twin tube shocks also have the added benefit of being inexpensive. Many companies produce twin tube shock absorbers for Land Rover, some of these are: Terrafirma, Britpart, Monroe, Super Gaz, and Old Man Emu. All of these will give a good service life and the Monroe will be the closest to a stock ride. Factory shocks can still be purchased but, for the price, I strongly recommend upgrading to a premium replacement.

The other type of shock for Land Rovers is the mono-tube design. Mono tube shocks are superior in every way except one; damage resistance. All it takes is one small dent in the mono tube shock and it is done for. Otherwise, mono tube shocks are very fade resistant, responsive and the ride quality is unbeatable.

Bilstein

The biggest advantage is their ability to dampen bounce and rebound which is the main purpose of a shock absorber. A mono-tube reacts much faster, stays much cooler, lasts longer and will almost never fade, even in the worst situations. These shocks are pricey (usually twice as expensive) but, in my opinion, are worth every penny. The top brand and probably the best shock made anywhere is Bilstein. Bilstein shocks will most likely be the last shock purchase for your vehicle. They have a lifetime warranty, are made specifically for each vehicle and have no springs or check valves to wear out.

Even though I am a huge fan of Bilstein, Old Man Emu has a new Nitrocharger Sport shock that I am very interested in. Old

Man Emu basically married both twin tube and mono tube designs to get a best of both worlds product. These have the twin tube ruggedness with the mono tube ride and dampening. The best part is they are $50.00 less expensive per shock than Bilstein and come in different levels of firmness.

I have also read many great reviews regarding Terrafirma's All Terrain shocks. Most are very happy with the ride and durability, and the best part is the price.

Monroe shocks can be found at any auto parts store. Bilstein, BritPart, Old Man Emu, and Terrafirma shocks will have to be purchased from a Land Rover specific dealer.

Springs

I wrote earlier of the benefits of long travel coil springs at each corner of a vehicle. Springs, however, do wear out and cause the vehicle to sag a bit. I see older Rovers all the time that sit so low they look like a Subaru. A new set of stock springs are not very expensive and will go a long way to restoring the ride quality and look your Rover is intended to have.

The aftermarket also caters to Land Rover owners with medium and heavy duty versions to compensate for winches, off road bumpers and towing. Of course there are 1 inch to 3 inch higher lift options as well, but I will go in to that later.

Some Rovers came, as an option, from the factory with adjustable rear air springs. It is a nice feature that allows drivers to raise the rear of the vehicle when off road for more ground clearance and it also self levels with heavy cargo or while towing. But, they were made of rubber, after a while would leak, and the compressor would not be able to keep the back end of the Rover aloft.

There are solutions. One could always replace the worn out air springs with new ones but this is expensive and not permanent, as these too will eventually leak. Most of the aftermarket Rover parts companies sell a kit that will allow you to replace the air springs with regular coil springs. These coil spring conversion kits last much longer, hold up to more abuse, and at a far lower price to boot.

 If you want to keep the adjustability of the air springs, Firestone and Air Lift make kits that will allow you to install much longer lasting urethane air bags inside the coil springs to achieve the same purpose. These come with Schrader valves that mount in the bumper allowing the air bags to be inflated just like a tire giving up to 1,000 lbs of leveling power. Both companies also make an inflation kit that can be controlled from inside the vehicle with an on board compressor and gages. Finally, some people have even hooked up the stock Land Rover compressor system to these new air bags for automatic control and leveling.

Suspension Bushings

A vehicle's suspension bushings will typically need to be replaced every 5 to 8 years, depending on where you live and how and where you drive. Road contaminates, salt, ozone or an arid climate will cause stock rubber bushings to crack and deteriorate. Some vehicles will see a substantial reduction in handling and performance in just three years of driving. I have talked to many people who have never heard of suspension bushings, much less that they wear and need to be replaced periodically.

Suspension bushings are located at every place where there is a joint or two connected pieces that have to allow for movement. Their purpose is to isolate road noise and remove vibration and harshness while allowing movement. To achieve this, most auto manufacturers use a fairly soft rubber which gives a nice supple ride but has the downside of allowing more deflection from the suspension, effectively allowing the alignment to change around corners and over bumps. As a bushing wears, it allows even more movement with the added annoyance of creaks and squeaks.

I recommend a much better bushing made from polyurethane. These are stiffer and more resilient than rubber and will typically last the life of the vehicle. I have never replaced a bushing on any vehicle that I have owned without it being polyurethane.

Most companies carry a lifetime warranty for their poly bushings and some even have different levels of stiffness. A company called Polybush makes full kits to replace all the bushing in your vehicle. These come in three different levels of hardness: Performance, Dynamic and Comfort.

If going with the Polybush brand, I recommend purchasing their Dynamic set or mid range as these will add some stiffness and performance to your suspension without being too harsh or noisy. The performance ones are designed just for that, performance and will stiffen the ride to a point that you will probably need to replace some bushings in your back as well, after a few miles. The Comfort line will restore the vehicle back to factory fresh feel but have the added benefit of longevity and slightly better handling.

Another manufacturer who makes a full bushing kit is Britpart. These come in bright-as-the-sun yellow or black and have a close to factory stiffness. The Britpart bushings however are about half as much money as the Polybush ones.

Britpart Bushing Kit

Most of these kits come with detailed instructions, can be installed by a novice and should take about a weekend. These are well worth the time and money and really transform your vehicle with improved handling, ruggedness and control.

Death Wobble

The death wobble is one of the scariest experiences a Land Rover owner can have. When a Discovery I or Range Rover Classic hits a rut, pothole or bunny, the vehicle tries to switch lanes or, at least, the steering wheel shakes violently enough to make you pull over and start over again. I hear of a lot of folks who start throwing parts at their Rover like: track rods, steering stabilizers, tie rod ends etc. but to no avail. These parts may help a little but the underlying problem is almost always the chassis bushings. Jeep Cherokees are also famous for this same problem with the same cure. Basically what happens is the worn bushings allow the front or rear axle to shift, sometimes rapidly. This causes the vehicle to abruptly switch lanes or start shaking violently.

Suspension Lifts

The first modification most people think of when they own a 4X4 is a lift kit. A typical lift for Land Rover vehicles is about two inches or 50mm and consists of new springs and shocks. The reasons for this modification is to gain ground clearance, allow for larger tires, and more off road prowess; also you get huge cool points.

One could lift their Rover very inexpensively by using spacers. These spacers are sold by almost all of the Land Rover specific parts stores listed at the beginning of this book. These spacers simply mount between the coil spring and axle, are typically made of solid aluminum, and will last the life of the vehicle.

To compensate for towing and cargo loads, most Land Rovers without rear air springs, sit higher in the rear than the front. A one inch spacer in the front will level the vehicle out and make it look much more rugged. This will also ensure the fitment of slightly larger tires like the 265/60 R

18. I did this and get asked all the time if I lifted it. I always get compliments on how my Rover it looks, usually by other Discovery drivers.

There are a few companies who make lift kits with shocks and springs, for Land Rover; they are Old Man Emu, Terrafirma and Britpart. All of these kits are priced fairly and do work, but from a mechanic's point of view, are missing a few necessities. When lifting a coil-sprung vehicle with straight axles, the front and rear axles pull inward toward the center of the vehicle and the front moves slightly to the left.

The biggest thing Rover drivers will notice is the vehicle not tracking down the road correctly, turning right better than it turns left and the steering wheel not returning to center as easily. Off road, drivers will also lose some of the possible approach and departure angles which will diminish the purpose of a lift in the first place.

I am of the opinion that if you are going to do something, you should do it right. Right consists of correcting all of the driveline angles; it also looks much better which is why most people get a lift in the first place. All of the companies I listed earlier sell new radius arms in the front and new trailing arms in the rear that will correct the caster by three degrees respectively. This pushes your front and rear axles back out to the ends of the vehicle where they belong.

The next thing that will need to be installed is an adjustable track rod. This will allow the front axle to be centered again under the vehicle and will allow the vehicle to turn both directions with happiness. Doing all of this will make your vehicle act and drive like it did before the lift.

Finally, the watts linkage is what keeps the rear axle from moving side to side but allows movement up and down for suspension travel. A Watts Linkage is a much better set-up than the traditional pan hard rod that most vehicles and Rover front ends come with, even though they do the same thing.

Watts Linkage

The problem: the Watts Linkage will hit its own mounting bracket when the axle hits full articulation, thus limiting said articulation. If this binding continues it will lead to fatigue and eventually failure. Although this usually will not happen unless a 3 inch lift is installed and the sway bar is disconnected. There is a solution though. A company called RTE produces sells a re-engineered Watts linkage which is much stronger and curved differently to prevent binding and allow full articulation.

One more consideration when lifting any vehicle is to replace the existing brake hoses with extended braided units. You definitely do not want the stock brake hoses to act as the limiting straps for your axles. The stock brake hoses are designed to allow the stock suspension to drop to its maximum. Adding two or three more inches of axle drop will cause the stock hoses to break, causing the brakes to fail.

In conclusion, to do a lift correctly one will spend roughly $1500.00 or more.

Tires

Tires are actually a part of the suspension system; they allow the vehicle to roll, provide traction and absorb shock. Like with most automotive parts, there are many different brands and types of tires available from many different companies. Unfortunately, tires have become very expensive over the last few years due to the fact that they use petroleum in their production and shipping. I wrote this section to help you make a good and economical choice.

Rover vehicles came from the factory with a basic all-season tread designed to work in most situations and with a standard load rating. These tires work well in rain and snow with good dry pavement grip, a nice ride, good longevity, and they are quiet. The only drawback is in off road situations. All season tires will easily pack with mud and the soft sidewalls that give that nice ride are susceptible to punctures from off road obstacles.

If you have the 16" wheels that were common from 1999 to 2002, your vehicle most likely came with 255/65 R16 sized tires, this equates to 29 x 10 inches. A Discovery will allow a slightly larger sizes of 255/70 R16 to help fill in those wheel wells and give you a bit more off road prowess. Some have installed as large as 265/70 R16 but with some rubbing at full turn and under articulation, although a one inch spacer should cure this.

Both of these larger sizes will fit as long as the springs are not sagging too much and if they are you should replace them anyway.

With the 18" wheels, the stock tire size is 255/55 R18 or again 29 X 10. The larger sizes would then be: 255/60 R18, which are hard to find and 265/60 R18 which are much more plentiful.

Here is a 265/60 R 18 installed on a Discovery II

Now, what about a 2" lift kit? Well, with a lift you can go a bit bigger, such as the 265/75 R16. For the 18" wheels, the same size would be 265/65 R18 or if you want a C or E load range tire with a mud option;
Go with the 275/65 R18.

These sizes seem to be the most popular sizes for stock and with a lift. There should be a couple things to keep in mind when choosing a tire size besides whether it fits or not. First is width. It is true that a wider tire looks cool and works better in some situations such as sand, mud and dry pavement, but it will be worse in wet and snowy conditions.

A wider tire displaces more of the vehicle's weight over a broader tread patch which causes the vehicle to float over sand and mud and allows more traction on dry pavement. In snowy or wet situations—skinny is better as it effectively slices through to the pavement instead of floating. Finally, there is a narrow tire option with the 16" wheel, it is the 235/70 R16 but the 18" wheels do not.

Now, we get into load range. Rover factory tires came in standard load which is considered a standard 4ply passenger tire. These will give Rovers a nice supple ride and handle a load of roughly 2000lbs which is way more than a Discovery can handle anyway.

The downside to these is off road puncture resistance and a low tread depth. The tread depth usually seen on a standard load tire is 12/32nds of an inch. For load range C,D, and E is around 16/32nds

The popular load range of years past for an on/off road vehicle was a C load range and are still prevalent in the 15" wheel sizes but unfortunately are not common with 16 or 18" wheels.

The C load range is a great all around tire. It has a nice ride, great puncture resistance and 16 to 18/32nds of an inch tread depth. If you find the tires you like in this load range, definitely get them. At the time of this writing, the only way to get a C load range is with a lift kit installed and 265/75/R16 or the 275/65/R18.

When you start to get into the larger sizes with lift kits, you will start to see D and E load ranges or 8 and 10ply tires. Some might think, the more the better, but this is not the case. D and E tires add more un-sprung weight and will diminish the way the vehicle handles and feels over bumps, not to mention the added stiffness of these tires will transfer every little bump right into your spine. These heavier tires will also hurt your gas mileage and acceleration.

An SL tire weighs about 35lbs; a D load range weighs about 50lbs and an E about 55lbs. It makes a big difference and the only benefit is better puncture resistance, load capacity and tread depth. Unless you have your heart set on a certain tire that only comes in these ranges, stick with standard Load.

Now we get into tread design. It seems everyone who wants to make their truck look more off road worthy will go get the gnarliest set of mud tires they can get their hands on. These tires are really only made for mud just like the name says, and that is where they shine. Most of them are sipe-less, which means that they do not have those little cuts in the tread. Sipes are very important for snow and ice traction and water too. They act like little fingers looking for and getting purchase over slippery surfaces. I have sold and installed a bazillion tires during my career and have many times had to talk a customer out of purchasing mud tires for the snow. They work well in deep snow that no one has driven on yet, but on packed snow, they might as well be bald.

Another thing, Mud tires have large voids between the tread blocks which allow them to clean the mud out of the tread and get more grip, almost like a paddle tire. These large voids cause much more rolling resistance, effectively killing your fuel mileage and power. The other side effect is road noise and in sand they will usually just dig a hole.

Don't get me wrong, they do have their place. If I were to go on a trek through an un-inhabited jungle, I would get the best set of mudders I could find too. But let's face it, most people drive their 4X4 on pavement 90% of the time and off road 10% of the time, so most should get a tire for this situation.

The tread design I am speaking of is an all terrain. An all terrain tire is designed to be useful in all but the stickiest of mud. They work great on the road, in snow and in most off road situations, plus they still look good.

If going off road is the farthest thing from your mind, I would stick with a good all season. These are truly built for all of that 90% on-road driving I was talking about.

They will give you the most longevity, best on-road traction and economy and will still work fine for some light four wheeling when needed.

Here are some of my recommendations:

The tire I recommend most for off road use and has, been released in many sizes that will fit a Discovery, is the Goodyear Wrangler

Good Year DuraTrac

DuraTrac. This tire is great in everything from mud to snow and looks aggressive too. These are not actually classified as an all terrain or a mud tire but called a commercial traction tire. These even have the mountain/snowflake symbol which guarantees great snow traction. And finally they have a full 16/32nds of tread depth in a Standard Load rated tire. The only drawback is that it will kill about one mile to the gallon and have a mild hum on the highway due to the more aggressive tread design.

General Grabber AT 2

For an all terrain tire, I would recommend the:

General Grabber AT2. It has the snowflake symbol for severe weather use and work really well in all situations. They are very reasonably priced as well. The only drawback to this type of tread design is their tendency to pack with mud.

I also really like the Toyo Open Country. Many manufacturers have recently started copying Toyo's 5 rib, heavily siped design because it has proven to be so effective in so many situations. This design will also allow the tires to self clean and push through mud a bit better than the generals.

Cooper Discovery ATP. This is a five rib design that I recently purchased from Discount Tire. They look aggressive and are reasonably priced. They are very quiet, as quiet as my street tires were and extremely confident off road. Cooper's sister tire, the AT3 is supposed to work just as well.

For an all season tire I would recommend the:

Continental Cross Contact LX20. This is, in my opinion, one of the best all season tire available. They have great tread wear, snow traction and low rolling resistance at a good price. They may even give you   some better gas mileage!

I also recommend replacing the spare tire when replacing the other four. I do have a good reason for this. The spare tire gets forgotten about until it is needed and when it is needed it is usually a half rotten, half flat relic from when the vehicle was new. Another reason; optimally, all of the tires on a vehicle should be the same model and size. Take two different tire manufacturers with the same size tire and you can find as much as an inch difference in diameter between the two.

This is a big deal on a Land Rover which is always in four wheel drive. A smaller diameter tire spins faster going down the road versus a larger one. From the vehicle's point of view, it has three tires going one speed and a fourth going another. This will cause excessive wear on the differential of the axle; the different size tire is mounted on. Furthermore, as tires wear from full tread to bald, roughly one inch of diameter will be lost.

Finally, rotating the spare tire into the standard rotation will give more wear to the set of tires and pay for itself through the extra mileage. Any tire shop worth their salt can do this procedure. Also, it is an absolute myth that a radial tire has to be run in the same direction its whole life. The only time this comes into play is with directional tires. So if your local tire shop tells you that you can't do a five way rotation; find a different tire shop. If you plan on doing your own rotations, a simple pattern to use is to just go round about with the tires. Just put the left rear wheel where the spare is, the spare where the right rear tire is, right rear to right front, right front to left front and so on. You can make up any pattern you like as long as you rotate them every 5000 miles.

Large Size Spare Tire Fitment

After you lift a Rover and upgrades to new, bigger tires, you will find that now you can't mount a full sized spare in the factory location. What happens is the spare tire now hits the top of the rear bumper.

Many people just throw the spare tire on top of their vehicle, although that is a much better place for cargo or luggage. Also, always having the spare tire on top will cause more wind resistance and cost fuel mileage. Fortunately for the big tire folks, there is a tire mounting bracket available from Atlantic British that will offset the Rover's spare tire upwards enough to accommodate up to 33 inches.

Cooling System

Antifreeze/Coolant

Unfortunately, Land Rover decided it would be a good idea to use the orange OAT style coolant that GM began using back in 1996. OAT stands for Organic Acid Technology and is formulated to last five years or 150,000 miles. Sounds good right?

It isn't all it is cracked up to be. OAT coolant has been accused of causing the famous intake manifold gasket leaks in most of the GM V6s.

Other things it has been blamed for include: coolant hose deterioration, aluminum corrosion, turning to mud when exposed to air, destroying the water pump, the list goes on and on. It is incompatible with green antifreeze to a point where it causes a severe chemical reaction, turning into a gelatinous goop and adding water will cut its life in half.

One of the big problems Rover engines sometimes have is head gasket failure and some say the coolant is to blame since it seems to eat gasket material. Well, a bad head gasket will allow the engine to burn or leak antifreeze and if driving a Discovery around with low coolant, the OAT will turn into the consistency and color of mud. It also tends to corrode the coolant reservoir cap which allows air into the system, causing the coolant again to turn to mud.

So the safe bet is to get rid of the OAT coolant and install something else. Some mechanics will suggest changing it all out and going with the classic green coolant, which actually does have superior aluminum protection and heat absorption. Or go with a Hybrid-OAT coolant (HOAT). The classic green coolant does do its job very well but has the drawback of needing to be changed every three years or 30,000 miles. Rover owners, who decide to go green, will want to flush the hell out of the system and get the entirety OAT out since it is not compatible.

My suggestion is to do a full system flush and use a Hybrid OAT or HOAT coolant. HOAT is completely compatible with all other coolants and has a longer service life and no drawbacks that I know of. This is the light yellow stuff.

Most auto repair shops have a coolant flush machine which will draw all of the coolant out of your vehicle and replace it with a recycled HOAT coolant and for a very reasonable price. Some might be a little reluctant to use any recycled fluid in their vehicle and I used to have the same feeling. Until I toured a facility that recycles coolant and from what I have seen, they do an amazing job of it and have a very good product. This is the coolant I have used in all of my vehicles for the last ten years.

Otherwise, do it your selfers are looking at draining the system, filling it with water, bringing it up to temperature, letting it cool down and draining it again. Do this procedure at least two times to get all the Dex out of the system before putting in the new coolant and then making sure to get the correct 50/50 mixture with the remaining water that will be trapped in the engine and heater core.

So, it really makes sense to just take it to a shop and have it done for about $100.00.

Hose Clamps

Rover coolant hoses sometimes leak or even completely blow off, especially while driving on the highway. If a bad head gasket is allowing exhaust to enter the coolant, pressure will build in the system and will definitely blow off a hose. The reason for this is the spring-pinch style hose clamps. Modern Land Rover engines run hot to begin with and do not deal well with overheating. There have been many stories of people blowing off a hose while driving down the freeway and destroying their engines very quickly. This happened to me (not the engine overheating but loosing a hose) luckily the hood was open and it was idling. My excess pressure was due to a bad head gasket. I will go over my recommendations for a head gasket replacement in the next section.

The cheap fix is to routinely check the hose clamps every oil change by pulling on the hose it is supposed to hold. A permanent fix is to replace all of the clamps with a high grade, screw type units from a local auto parts store. This is time consuming and messy since the hoses have to be removed to replace the clamps and are full of coolant. At the minimum, upgrade the hose clamps when replacing the hoses or when the system is drained.

Air in the Cooling System

Reading some of the Land Rover forums, I am amazed at how many people have a hard time getting the air out of their cooling system. Air in a Land Rover's cooling system can cause all kinds of problems due to the location of the coolant temp sensor. If an air bubble gets trapped at this sensor, the computer has no idea what temperature the engine is in its current state. This can cause hard starting, misfires at idle and the dumping of way too much fuel through the engine. Another indicator of air in the cooling system is what sounds like someone flushing a toilet upon acceleration.

It is a simple procedure but, make sure the engine is not hot:

1. There is a bleeder valve located at the top of the engine where the coolant hoses come together. Simply loosen this bleeder about two full turns.

2. Now, pull up on the coolant reservoir until it detaches.

3. Hold the reservoir up as high as it will go and add the coolant to the system.

4. Continue this until nothing but coolant comes out of the bleeder. Without lowering the reservoir, tighten the bleeder, DO NOT over tighten as it will break and you will have to replace the whole upper hose assembly to fix it..

5. Now re-install the reservoir and replace the cap. You are done.

Cooling System Bleeder Screw

Coolant Leaks

There are a lot of jokes about British vehicles and leaks, but Land Rovers are not that bad. They do, however, have a few places they leak coolant. One of the most common places is at the throttle body pre-heater gasket. The throttle body pre-heater is designed to keep the throttle from freezing in cold climates. It does this by running coolant through a plate attached to the bottom of the throttle body. If you notice coolant on the left bank valve cover, this is probably the culprit.

There is an easy kit to install by you and it is fairly inexpensive to purchase from Atlantic British. This kit will come with a new heater plate, gasket and screws.

Another place for leaks is from the head gaskets. Typically when a head gasket goes on a Land Rover, it will leak coolant from one of the heads and down the back of the engine. I have a write up with suggestions for head gaskets in the engine section of this book.

Under Hood Temperatures

With the combination of a high temperature thermostat, aluminum engine block and unshielded exhaust, modern Land Rovers have ridiculously high under hood temperatures. This causes quite a few of the common problems Land Rovers are known for. Some of these problems include: melted wires, especially the ones that run to the right side of the engine, coolant hose failure, vacuum hose failure, head gaskets, ignition coil and wire failure, and the destruction of anything not made of metal.

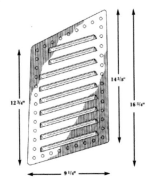

A very effective fix for this is to vent the hood to pull some of the heat out. There are a few different solutions out there to get this done. One option and in my opinion a good looking one, is to install louvered vents. I saw a set sold by Rocky Road Outfitters on a Discovery at a car show. The owner told me that his under hood temperatures dropped by over 80 degrees on average, after he installed them. The scariest part of this solution is cutting holes in the hood, so I strongly recommend having it done at a professional body shop.

Check out Rocky Road Outfitters for louvered hood vents.

Another area to address is the thermostat. A thermostat is a simple on/off switch just like the one on the wall in your house. It is designed to stop or slow coolant flow until the engine reaches operating temperature and then keep it there.

In my opinion, Rovers run a little hot for the old tech design of the engines. A Rovers' stock thermostat opens at 212 degrees and closes at 202 degrees Fahrenheit. The main reason for this is to get the Rover V8 to pass modern emissions standards. Some aftermarket companies have addressed this with a warm weather thermostat that opens closer to a more rational 190 degrees Fahrenheit. This cooler thermostat is also known to help with the "knocking at idle" problem the later model Discoverys are known for. I purchased one of these from Atlantic British and it is fairly easy to install.

Find Warm Weather Thermostats at Atlantic British

Finally, the under hood wiring will need some protection as well. On the Discovery, there is a large part of the wiring harness on the right side of the engine compartment that sits just above the exhaust manifold. This group of wires gets hit with so much heat that the plastic tubing covering them and eventually the wire insulation itself deteriorates and falls off. This then allows the electrical gremlins that Land Rover has been known for.

Main Wiring Harness Wrapped With Header Insulation

There is a simple solution, and that is to protect the wires from the heat. Something the factory should have done in the first place.

Summit Racing Equipment and many auto parts stores have heat insulation tape that is good up to 1100 degrees, will keep the wires cool and intact. Simply pull off all the old convoluted tubing and wrap all the wires with the tape. The convoluted tubing is usually so cooked that it just crumbles away. I actually used a header wrap and zip ties to protect mine just because I already had them lying around and knew it would work. Go through the engine compartment and find any wires that have the factory wire covers cooked away and at least wrap them in electricians tape if not the insulation tape.

Engine

Engine Knocking at Idle

This knocking usually happens when the engine is warm and at idle. It sounds as if someone is hitting the side of the block it with a large hammer. It is usually louder underneath the vehicle and goes away under acceleration.

Do not confuse this sound with a light clicking noise in the front top of the engine (serpentine belt tensioner or idler pulley). The cause of the real problem is that some of the cylinder liners are moving up and down with the pistons inside the engine.

Rover V8s are an all aluminum design with a cast iron sleeve pressed into the cylinder bore for wear purposes. Unfortunately, Land Rover used a cheap tapered tube sleeve and worn out equipment when they built the last of these engines. The worn out equipment made the bore holes in the block out of tolerance, allowing a looser fit of the sleeve thus allowing them to move.

This problem tends to be more common in the 4.6L engines made in 2003/04 than the 4.0s of earlier years. Just as a side note, I had this problem when I purchased my vehicle and did the cheap solution below. I have not had any problems since, no catastrophic failures, nothing; and I use my Discovery for everything even towing on long road trips.

The best and permanent solution is to have top hat cylinder liners installed in the block. This will permanently cure this problem and give a lot of longevity out of the engine.

Top Hat Cylinder Liners

Unfortunately, in order to install them you are looking at a full engine rebuild or I should say, you might as well rebuild if they are going to be installed. Just do not do an engine rebuild without them.

Also, if going the engine rebuild route, choose an engine re-builder who knows these engines very well. A good place to find a competent rebuilder of the rover engine is to check with a local, independent Rover repair shop and find out who they use. Too many times, I have heard of mistakes while cutting the space for the top hat cylinder liners and destroying the block. Now, you are typically left without an engine because most of these engine rebuilders will just say "sorry" and refund your money for their services.

The preferred option is to go with a fully rebuilt engine from many of the Rover specific parts houses listed at the beginning of this book. These engines are pre run to break the camshaft in correctly, checked for everything and have a nice warranty.

Top Hat Cylinder Liners are not easy to find. Try Paddock Spares and Accessories in the U.K.
www.paddockspares.com

Another solution, and this is not a permanent solution to the core of the problem but, it does make the noise go away and keep the sleeves from moving around. The first thing to do is to install an oil cooler. Since the 4.0 wasn't plagued, nearly as much, with this problem and the only change was a longer stroke and the removal of the oil cooler, I thought it might be the way to go.

Like with most things, Land Rover got rid of the oil cooler but left the oil pump unchanged, so folks can plug the aftermarket oil cooler hoses into the stock locations. This sounds easy but you will have to find the correct hose barbs to replace the plugs.

The easy rout is to go with a sandwich style oil cooler adapter. These simply fit between the engine and oil filter and have two ports to feed oil to the cooler and then back to the engine. Some of these adapters also have the added benefit of a 180 degree thermostat built in for cold weather warm up. They are sold in kits from Summit Racing Equipment and Jegs Performance and come with everything included for a nice easy installation.

Another option, albeit, untried by me, is to get a stock oil cooler from a salvage yard. The 2002 and earlier models were equipped with these and it is a nice design. Then just install it in the stock place. With an oil cooler installed, start using a high quality 5w30 engine oil like Valvoline Max Life. Land Rover recommends using 10w40 which by today's standards is pretty thick. I figured the higher viscosity would cause a bit more viscous friction between the piston and sleeve, causing movement. Well I think I was right and have not heard a peep out of my engine since.

I did, however, put 10w40 back in at one of my oil changes a few thousand miles later and the noise returned. So the key seems to be using the thinner oil.

I do have a couple more recommendations, especially if the noise did not abate. Use an aftermarket "warm weather" thermostat from Atlantic British. The idea is that the aluminum block and cylinder liners expand differently when heated, allowing the sleeves to loosen in their bores and move. Therefore, cooling the engine down will help keep a grip on the sleeves. I actually tried this first, after a local Rover enthusiast told me about it and it did not completely handle the problem but, did lessen it. That is when I realized that the knock didn't start when the engine coolant warmed up but when the oil did.

Atlantic British carries Warm Weather Thermostats

Lastly and just for good measure, use an upper cylinder lubricant like Marvel Mystery Oil or Lucas in the fuel. These have many more benefits than just lubricating the upper cylinder walls. It will also lubricate the fuel pump and injectors; plus they keep everything nice and clean.

Head Gaskets

Land Rovers usually kill their head gasket at about 100,000 miles and throughout this book I have given my opinion on some of the reasons why. Another reason and again in my opinion, is the newer engines use a composite gasket with those one-time-use-only elastic head bolts. I have never been a fan of these head bolts, main shaft bolts or the use of any bolt as a high torque fastener. The problem is, when torque is applied to a head bolt it has to deal with multiple forces, not just the lateral force of holding the head down. In my opinion these weaken over time (about 100,000 miles) and allow the head gasket to leak. Also, they are a huge pain in the butt to torque down since they are torqued by degrees of rotation instead of a torque wrench setting. One last point on my rant is that not all head bolts are created equally. I have replaced head gaskets in other brands of vehicles in the past and have had a bad batch of replacement head bolts fail; making me do the job over again.

A permanent solution is the use of ARP head studs. These studs are installed only hand tight before any torque is applied; therefore they only have lateral clamping force with no added twisting force. These studs are of the highest quality material and almost never fail. Another great benefit is the clamping force over the head is much more even. I could sing the praises of head studs through the rest of this book and have never met a race engine builder who did not use them. They are only about twice the price of replacement head bolts if you purchase from Lucky 8 and are reusable.

ARP Head Stud Kit

When installing the head studs on some Land Rovers, there may not be enough room to get the heads over the studs. If this is the case, lay the head on the block and gasket, install the studs just like the bolts with the head in place, finger tighten then install the washers and nuts and torque per the instructions. Make sure, when replacing the head gaskets, that you get the heads milled and the valve seals replaced.

Purchase ARP Head Studs from Lucky 8 for the best price.

Engine Replacement

Occasionally, an engine kicks the bucket even with religious maintenance and some of my tips and tricks. Sometimes a hose blows off and the engine catastrophically over heats or a rock rips through the oil pan and all the oil is lost. When this happens there are two choices to make:

- Sell your Land Rover. This can be a good choice for some who are sick of the "personality" of their Land Rover. Others might sell it due to the numbers. A mint condition Discovery II will sell for roughly the same amount as a rebuilt engine from most parts places.

Or

- Replace the engine. The same Discovery, with a bad engine, will usually sell for  less than $2000.00. If the Land Rover in question is in good shape otherwise, then an engine replacement should be a strong consideration. If one looks at the purchase costs of a new or even a serviceable, used vehicle, verses the recoup price of a broken Discovery, a replacement engine again looks like a good option. Plus, most rebuilt engines use better than original parts and top-hat cylinder liners to make a very reliable unit that should last well past 200,000 miles. For me, I would much rather keep my ultra capable, super cool and comfortable Land Rover for another ten years rather than drive a reliable, over priced Toyota that can be seen on every street corner.

Oil Leaks

British vehicles are famous for two things, style and leaking oil. Fortunately, Land Rovers usually only leak oil from the valve cover gaskets. Before I replaced mine, I was losing a quart of oil every 1000 miles through these gaskets. The OEM valve cover gaskets were only good for about the first 30,000 miles. Another contributing factor is the old style GM four bolt valve covers themselves. Older GM V8s designed in the same era had this same problem. Thankfully, the aftermarket has come through with very workable replacement gaskets made of soft rubber that last. On the modern Bosch engines this is not an easy job as the upper intake plenum must be removed to access the valve covers. If ever the ignition cables or coil are being replaced, make sure to replace the valve cover gaskets as well. There may still be some seepage from other gaskets but most will not be that severe and can be handled with high mileage oil.

Good Valve Cover Gaskets can be found through most of the Land Rover specific parts stores

Exhaust

Land Rover exhaust systems are actually well designed. My Discovery has a 2 into 1 design with easy flowing mandrel bends and a 2.5 inch pipe diameter after the Y pipe. Also, the exhaust manifolds are a quality, cast iron, shorty header design that dump into two high quality catalytic converters.

Happily, there are some cheap fixes and modifications that can be made to this very well designed system to eek out a bit more power and economy. Not to mention some much less expensive repairs.

Magnaflow Cat-Back Exhaust System

What I want to go over first, without getting too complicated is flow verses velocity. I am sure while driving around; you have seen modified cars and trucks with nothing short of a sewer pipe sized exhaust system hanging under their vehicle. It is annoyingly loud and surprisingly ineffective. The larger the pipe the less velocity and velocity will give more torque and horsepower in the lower rpm range of the engine. The Rover V8 makes all of its power below 4600 RPM, so a huge exhaust would actually hurt more than help.

Muffler

Shortly after I purchased my Discovery the muffler split down the seam. So I replaced it with a straight through design from Hooker Headers. Before I did this, I priced a stock replacement and found it to be way more than I wanted to pay.

Even though the muffler I chose is a straight through design, my vehicle did not get much louder and I was left with a nice low rumble.

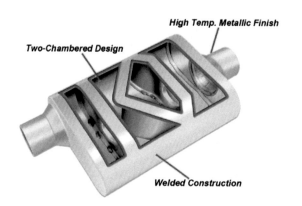

Thrush Welded Muffler

I do recommend keeping the resonator at the back of the exhaust system. The stock resonator will not cause any restrictions and will go a long way in quieting the exhaust down.

Unfortunately, after towing my 3500lb camping trailer 2000 miles last summer, my new muffler fell apart internally.

Resonator

I ended up installing the Thrush Welded muffler as a temporary replacement until I could order another Hooker (muffler). I was so impressed with the power gain, throatier sound, better fuel mileage, and indestructibility, that I will never take it off. I strongly recommend this muffler for the Discovery, it cost less than $40.00 and can be purchased at almost any auto parts store.

The muffler from Land Rover, like most stock factory units is a dog leg design, great for noise abatement but not flow.

There are a few other muffler designs out there, but be careful with which brand you choose, they are not all created equal. Many inexpensive mufflers will typically use the same internal pipe sizes for a 2" and a 3" muffler and can actually lose flow and horsepower, all that is gained is noise.

I have unfortunately also seen some expensive mufflers with poorly designed internals, small pipes and bad restrictions. I recommend the following:
- Hooker Headers' Max Flow

- Dynomax Ultra Flo and Super Turbo
- Anything made by Borla
- Thrush Welded
- Summit Racing Mufflers.

I have experience with all of these brands and models and have never once seen a bad example; they all have large flow tubes, superior quality construction and very nice results.

Still, when buying a muffler, I strongly recommend looking down the inlet and outlet pipes for any poor construction before you install, even with the pricey brands.

The most common designs are a turbo or reverse flow, glass pack, chambered and straight through. A turbo muffler will usually be the quietest. If going with a high quality one like the Dynomax Super Turbo or Summit's Turbo muffler these should have plenty of flow for Rover engines.

Next up we have the glass pack design and almost every muffler company makes one. Glass packs are usually the least expensive muffler you can find and are very tough but they are also very heavy and there is a need to be very careful of core sizes and type with these. Most glass packs I have seen in a 2.5 inch have a small 2.25 inch or even a 2 inch core. Also, glass packs come with two different core types. One is a perforated design which is basically a pipe with a bunch of holes punched in it (this is the better type). The other is a louvered design which has louvers that dip into the exhaust stream and cause turbulence that slows velocity and flow.

Many people in the performance world like the chambered muffler design, which basically has some welded plates inside that trap sound. These do seem to work very well for producing horsepower and they have the benefit of working as an anti-reversion device, keeping the exhaust moving in one direction.

Another big plus to the chambered muffler is that they are nearly indestructible and have no sound deadening material to blow out or disintegrate. The big drawback to this type is that they are loud and typically have a very annoying resonance but, if the resonator is not removed this will not be a problem.

The last design is the straight through Mufflers from Hooker or Dynomax. These actually do a decent job of canceling noise with little restriction but do tend to be the most expensive and also slightly less durable, compared the chambered type.

Installing a new after market muffler is a rather simple project. Tools you will need are: A Sawsall, hacksaw or some way of cutting through metal, a Sawsall will make it much easier. A welder always comes in handy for any exhaust work and it is highly recommended to weld your joints if you do any off roading. That is it for tools, now you just need a muffler, extension pipe, an exhaust hanger and three exhaust clamps. An aftermarket muffler will almost always be shorter in length than the stock muffler, in this case by about 12 inches.

Crawl under your vehicle and you will see how simple this job is. The only tricky part is working out your exhaust hangers. I reused mine by cutting them off just short of the welds and then re-welded them to the muffler. If a welder is not handy, then a universal hanger from an auto parts store can be used. Cut your muffler off at both ends where the exhaust pipes swell back to 2.5 inches then remove your muffler.

Now measure the extra length you will need and cut your extension pipe to suit. The extension pipe should be the type with one end at 2.5 inches inside diameter to fit over your existing pipe and the other at 2.5 inches outside diameter to slide in to your new muffler.

Now just pop everything together and weld and or clamp it, I usually do both for off road durability. One thing that will make this step much easier is to disconnect the tailpipe exhaust hanger at the rear, for more movement. Now hang everything back up and you are ready to roll.

Catalytic Converters

Now-a-days catalytic converters are much better built and fairly free flowing compared to their earlier versions. If they fail, which they do occasionally, they will put a stop to your driving. When a catalytic converter fails, it usually plugs up and stops allowing the exhaust to leave the engine. This failure is normally caused by contaminants in the fuel or oil, not keeping the ignition system in tune or even bad oxygen sensors pushing too much fuel through them. Also, if the check engine light is on or especially flashing, there is a possibility that damage could be occurring to the catalytic converters. I have even seen mice build nests in the exhaust systems of stored vehicles causing failures.

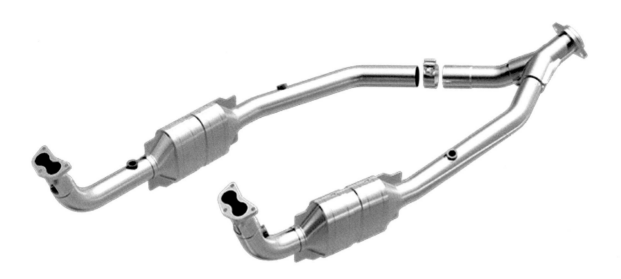

Magnaflow Catalytic Converters

Most vehicles only burn about 25% of the fuel in their tanks; the remaining fuel is used to quench the flame and cool the combustion chamber. A catalytic converter is used to burn as much of this extra fuel as possible to keep emissions down. Not very efficient, huh?

If you end up with a bad catalytic converter, you can go with a stock replacement one, which comes with both converters and the Y pipe and will cost one of your children. Thankfully, there are other options.

First thing to do is check the warranty. Manufacturers are required to have extended warranties on the catalytic system which makes it free or at least a lot cheaper. The warranty Land Rover gives this system a 50,000 miles. If your warranty has expired, Magnaflow makes an identical set up to stock with the added benefit of high flow catalytic converters for a decent price. Or the least expensive way to go, if you have to foot the bill, is to go with two new universal converters from Walker or

Magnaflow for about $100.00 each. Both of these have higher flow rates than stock and can be replaced just like a muffler.

Magnaflow also makes a full catalytic converter to tail pipe, performance, kit that will easily bolt right in. This really isn't necessary due to the high quality of the stock exhaust system (except the muffler of course.) This is a great option if your exhaust is rotting away or your catalytic converters are also bad.

Another point I would like to reiterate before ending this section is the check engine light. If ever the check engine light is flashing, **PULL OVER** as soon as possible. This flashing check engine light is telling you that too much unburned fuel is entering the catalytic converters and is doing damage to them.

Drive Train

Front Driveshaft

One of Land Rover's most famous problems is the front driveshaft. The universal joints in these are not serviceable and therefore cannot be greased on a regular basis. Inevitably the driveshaft will fail and with its proximity to the aluminum transmission, it will cost one of these too.

When the universal joint fails, the driveshaft hangs on to the front axle and becomes a big steel baseball bat, effectively knocking a fist size hole in the side of the transmission.

On top of being unserviceable, the driveshaft is also very close to the very hot catalytic converter on the right side, which bakes the grease in the universal joints. If that wasn't bad enough, the air conditioning will also drip water right on top of this poor U-joint.

Thankfully, there is a warning. Before this catastrophe happens and there will usually be a chirping noise from the front of the vehicle, **HEED THIS WARNING IMMEDIATELY** and call a tow truck!

Front Driveshaft

Most Rover parts companies sell fully serviceable replacement front driveshaft for Land Rovers for about the price of a stock one and most use heavy duty parts. Another solution is to go to the local drive line shop and have one built. The only problem with having it built is the situation of being without a vehicle for a few days.

To maintain this new driveshaft, grease all of the zirks at every oil change.

Rotoflex Joint

The rear driveshaft on the Land Rover is connected to the rear axle by what is called a rotoflex or rag joint instead of a universal joint like on most other vehicles.

A rotoflex joint has its upside which is providing a smooth, quiet application of torque but, for drivers who like to go off road or have a lift, steep driveline angles will destroy this joint fairly quickly. When this joint fails, owners are essentially left with a front wheel drive Land Rover and that is if they are lucky to have a locking center differential.

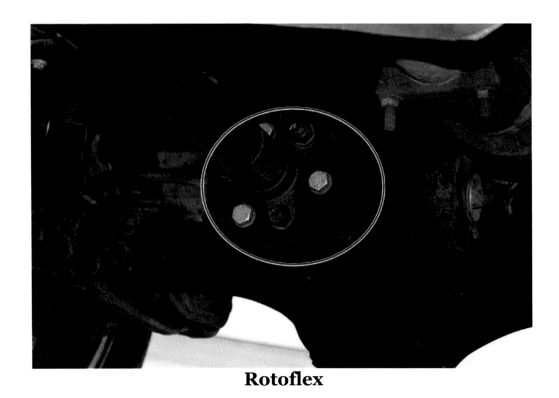

Rotoflex

There are a couple things that can be done. The first is to carry a spare rotoflex; they are fairly inexpensive, easy to install, and fit in the glove box. Make sure it is a genuine Land Rover part or an aftermarket equivalent to the original, as some of these have been recalled due to failure in the past.

The most durable rout is to replace the rotoflex completely with a replacement U-joint driveshaft. This replaces the rotoflex with a standard, serviceable, driveshaft universal joint that will hold up to almost anything. This is a must for anyone with a lift kit installed.

Purchase either a new Rotoflex joint or the universal joint driveshaft from Toddco Suspension.

Non-Locking Center Differential

Land Rover figured that with the four channel traction control effectively giving a four wheel limited slip that Rovers no longer needed a locking center differential. In some ways, I can see the redundancy but there is a big difference between driving a locked center differential and a non-locked one when off road or in deep snow.

The center differential has to allow slippage between the front and rear axles to prevent binding on dry pavement. When in slippery situations, it tries to send all of the power to the axle with the least grip. Unlocked and in a slick or off road situation, the traction control goes nuts trying to keep the power going to all four wheels. While locked, the driver gets an even 50/50 transference of power to both front and rear axles.

All years between 1999 and 2003 came without a locking center differential, even though 1999 to 2001 had the internals but came without the lever to activate it. The 2004 model year was lucky enough to get the full set up with a lockable high and low range.

For the 1999 to 2001 Rover, owners can simply replace the lever and cable. This comes as a kit from a few manufacturers and is a fairly easy retrofit. With a 2002 or 2003, unfortunately the whole transfer case will have to be replaced. In this case, the least expensive route is to find a used transfer case from a Discovery I, earlier D II or a 2004 Discovery II in a junk yard and then purchase the cable and lever kit. If a junked 2004 Discovery is located both transfer case and lever can be had at a low price.

Land Rover transfer cases are a pretty bullet proof all gear design and will typically have a lot of life left when used even if they have been neglected. The main things to check for are off road damage and cracks in the case.

Instead of hitting the junkyard, Toddco Suspensions has re-sealed, lockable transfer cases for sale. For vehicles that are running larger tires, Toddco also has other options with lower gearing to make up for the loss in power. They also sell the diff lock lever, which is needed for the conversion.

A great place to purchase a diff lock lever is either Toddco or Lucky 8. Lucky 8 also has a how-to video for the installation of the lever on You Tube.

Pinion Carrier

All US destined Discoverys came equipped with a weak, two pinion carrier design in the differentials. They will hold up fine for normal use, towing and even some serious trail rides but, the small cross pins were prone to breakage when subjected to hard core off road use and oversized tires.

I have been pretty tough on mine so far, with no drama.

Thankfully, Land Rover has been recognized by some of the mainstream aftermarket drive train companies, such as ARB and Detroit Locker who make new aftermarket differentials that will eliminate any weakness in your axle. These aftermarket differentials are also limited slip or locking for much more traction.

Detroit True Trac By Eaton

Lockers

The Detroit Locker is world famous for durability, traction and unfortunately an annoying binding and tire chirp around corners.

Lockers work mechanically and lock while in a straight line and under power to give the vehicle 100% power to both wheels on an axle, even with one wheel in the air.

The ARB Air Locker is a selectable locker which gives that full locker traction while in the dirt without being a pain on the street. When turned off the ARB acts just like the stock-open differential, just tougher. Another plus point for the ARB is that you will have to install an onboard air compressor. These come in handy for re-inflating tires on the trail.

Limited Slip

Limited slip differentials, like the Detroit TruTrac, pre load the axles to allow full traction to both wheels, until one tire lifts off the ground then most of the power goes to the one in the air. This is not a huge problem with these vehicles since Discovery has a very well designed traction control system that will put on the brakes at the wheel with no grip, effectively making the TruTrac act like a locker. The best part about a limited slip differential is that they will not bind on the street. Even with the Discovery's awesome traction control, a limited slip or locking differentials will still provide a noticeable upgrade in off road prowess.

I know I went a little off topic here, but as a fix for the weak carrier, any of these differentials are basically indestructible.

Axle Shafts

The axle shafts on a Land Rover become the weak link after the replacement of the two pin carrier. Rover axle shafts are slightly weaker than the Dana 35 axles found on the front of many Jeeps. More than adequate for a stock vehicle, but with big upgrades in horsepower or tire size, add some hardcore four wheeling, these can fail.

KAM produces replacement, aerospace grade axle shafts and are sold through Terrafirma . These are 95% stronger and will handle just about anything that can be thrown at them and laugh.

Maintenance

In this section, I will go over any maintenance that has not been covered in the previous sections. Included will be recommendations for products and intervals for changing them. Most of the recommended maintenance procedures also include an upgrade as a normal course of action.

Lube Oil and Filter

Oil gets dirty from external and internal pollutants; also every brand has an additive package that will wear out eventually. This additive package helps keep the engine sludge free and the wear down. The same thing happens to the grease in the serviceable parts of the drive train; this is the lube part of lube oil and filter. The Filter is the oil filter, which clogs after awhile and will eventually allow the oil to be bypassed and unfiltered.

Oil is one of the most contentious subjects in the automotive world. Just go online and you will find whole forums on the subject of which oil is the best and which oil is the worst. Actually you will see the same percentages of people saying that brand A is way better than brand X as brand X is way better than brand A. It is pretty entertaining but not very useful. The truth is, the major and a lot of the minor motor oil companies employ engineers who know what they are doing and have nice budgets for research and development.

I am usually a firm believer in following the recommendations of the people who engineered the vehicle for most fluid changes. Although Land Rover specifically recommends using Castrol 10w40 oil in the Discovery, you do not necessarily need to use the recommended brand or weight. In fact I have found it beneficial to use lighter weight oil as mentioned earlier.

I have seen many oil tests, have received back many oil analyses from used motor oil and have torn apart many engines and found that most oils stack up pretty well against each other. Although, there are a few bad brands of oil out there, which are not to specification, and will harm an engine. Some of these will even have the API stamp on the back of the bottle. There is a group called The Petroleum Quality Institute of America and they are dedicated to "busting" these bad oil brands.

Check your next oil purchase on there website: www.pqiamerica.com

You are free to use whatever brand you like and will probably have satisfactory results. There are some store brand oils such as 7 Eleven or any auto parts store brand that are actually good oil. But, I usually recommend most people go with the major brand of oil such as: Valvoline, Mobile, Pennzoil, or Quaker State and your engine will live a long happy life. Pick a brand and stick with it. Sometimes two different additive packages from two different oil manufacturers will not be compatible and will cause sludge problems. Same goes with quick lube places; one will use Valvoline and another Pennzoil so pick one oil change place and stick with it as well.

I do recommend using high-mileage oil, because Land Rovers tend to leak a bit. There is that old adage, "If there is no oil under them then there is no oil in them," and I have seen that to be true on a few British makes. The other reason to use high mileage oil is the fact that it has a lot more ZDDP in it which keeps our flat tappet camshafts happy. I use Valvoline Max Life 5W30 and Here are my reasons: I live in Colorado where we get temperature swings from below zero to above 100° Fahrenheit; sometimes it seems in the same day. Max Life is semi-synthetic oil which will bolster its high temperature abilities and help it flow better when cold.

Finally, the additive package used in high mileage oils has a seal conditioner which causes all of the seals in the engine to swell between 8 and 10%. This will slow the hemorrhaging of the engine and since the last Discovery II was made in 2004, I doubt there are many with less than 75,000 miles which is when this type of oil is recommended.

I do not normally go against the manufacturer's recommendations for engine oil weights but, I have found 5W30 to both cure the engine knock at cold start up and at idle when warm. There is also the point that 90% of engine wear occurs at start up, thinner oil will flow much easier when cold, and get to all the parts that need it. Land Rover actually recommends 5W30 at temperatures below 80 degrees Fahrenheit in our engines.

I believe that thick 10W40 is recommended due to the lack of oil cooler and the looser tolerances Rover engines were constructed with. Some might be worried about 5W30 maxing out at a 30 weight in hot weather. For this Mobile 1 does make a synthetic 0w40 that will also work well but does not contain high amounts of ZDDP and will be more expensive. Or just add an oil cooler and run the 5W30 year round like I have. My engine has been much happier and trouble free as well

Oil Filter

There is a myriad of oil filters to choose from when at the parts store and, this is a purchase where you get what you pay for. Most high quality oil filters will have an anti-drain back valve, which keeps the oil from draining out of the engine and back into the oil pan when the engine is turned off. These valves keep dry start up and wear to a minimum.

Fram Ultra Synthetic

Also, the filter media in a quality filter will remove much smaller particles and retain its ability to filter longer. My recommendations are Wix, Bosch, K&N and Mobile 1. Fram also has a new filter out called the Ultra Synthetic; it is relatively inexpensive and very well built. After pulling one of these apart and seeing the quality that went into these; I have switched to this for all of my vehicles.

Finally, never do an engine oil flush on a Rover. These engines can be leaky in the first place and an engine flush will usually make it worse. Most of the engine flush products I have seen on the market are just a quart of diesel fuel. It does work, but it removes all of the build up around your gaskets and seals causing more leaks. I once did this on my old 1964 T-Bird and went from a slow leak at the main seals to losing about a quart of oil every ten miles or so. The oil additive package will keep the engine clean enough.

If sludge is a problem, add a quart of Marvel Mystery Oil or Sea Foam at the next few oil changes. Marvel Mystery Oil and Sea Foam have added solvents in them that will help with the sludge without causing leaks.

After talking about Marvel Mystery Oil and Sea Foam in this book the next paragraph is going to put my own foot in my mouth.

Another no-no is the use of most after market oil additives. Some people are firm believers in some brand or another to make their oil better but, no vehicle manufacturer has ever recommended one. Trust your oil brand; they know what they are doing.

Finally, I have found many Land Rover owners who like to use Rotella T6 15W40 diesel oil. Rotella is considered to be one of the best diesel oils on the market and has a great additive package (for diesels.) I do not recommend this, nor does Shell (the maker of Rotella.) The first reason; it is to high viscosity, will not flow sufficiently at start up, and cause heat build up from internal fluid friction. The second; it has way more ZDDP than you will ever need in a gasoline engine, which will destroy the catalytic converters. And finally, diesel oils have more additives per volume than their gasoline counter parts. Most of these additives are detergents which a diesel needs to handle all of the soot, blow by, and combustion byproducts they produce. These detergents will do their job in a gasoline engine and succeed at cleaning your cylinder walls to the point of lost compression. Also the materials used in the construction of the rover V8 where never designed to tolerate these additives and some will even eat away at the aluminum. Our poor engines have enough problems, use gasoline engine oil.

ZDDP

A question I get a lot is: What about the lack of ZDDP in modern oil with the flat tappet camshafts Land Rovers use?

ZDDP is actually Zinc dialkyldithiophosphates and is a high pressure anti-wear additive that has recently been reduced in most engine oil. The reason for the reduction is that ZDDP is thought to contaminate the catalytic converters which nowadays are covered by a long, if not lifetime, warranty.

The problem is, this additive was very important for flat tappet camshafts, which Rovers have and there is a fear that they will actually wear out.

Oil companies thought this through and modern oil does still protect flat tappet cams, but just barely. If you have a hardcore cam you will need quite a bit ZDDP or if you replace your camshaft you will need it for the break in period. A great solution and one I recommend for Rover engines anyway, is to always use a high quality, high mileage oil like Valvoline Max Life. The reason is for the "Friction Modifiers" advertised on the front of the bottle. This is ZDDP and about 50% more than what you get in conventional oil. ZDDP additives and performance oil with extra ZDDP are also available over the counter but tend to be really expensive

Spark Plugs

Occasionally, spark plugs and ignition wires will have to be replaced. Like oil, spark plug brands and design cause a lot of debate in the automotive enthusiast world. There are many companies out there making spark plugs like:

- Bosch
- NGK
- Champion

- Autolite
- Nippondenso

And with:

- Single
- Double
- Quadruple
- Diamond shaped grounds

Then you have:

- Copper
- Silver
- Platinum,
- Iridium
- Pulse plugs
- V electrodes.

So what is a Land Rover owner to do? Well, you can always use the plugs the factory installed and they will work fine for the full service interval.

You might ask yourself, "With all of these options out there, maybe something will work better than stock." Every engine make that I have come across has its own personality; they either love a modification or hate it and some make no difference at all.

I have also seen a certain spark plug do fine in one engine and the same brand barely keep another make running.

Most plugs seem to work okay in the Rover V8 but the consensus, per the online forums, seems to be the Bosch Platinum +4. It works really well and gives a Rover a bit more pep and economy. I personally have never seen these plugs do poorly. Others say that the E3 plugs work really well. Some swear by the plain old copper core Champion's.

A copper core plug will need to be changed about every 30,000 miles, platinum, about 60 to 80,000 and iridium 100,000.

The plugs I recommend the most are the stock plugs. Unfortunately, stock plugs are no longer available in the US. One of my personal favorites for Land Rover engines are the Denso PK16TT Platinum TT Spark Plug. These are very durable, have great performance and are much less expensive than the fancy design or iridium plugs. Iridium plugs from most manufacturers will give long life and great performance but at a premium price.

Ignition Wires

Rover engine compartments get very hot and most ignition cables deteriorate and fail in short order. There are only a few ignition cables that will handle the heat and last a normal service interval. Trust me; you do not want to do this job more times than have to. In order to change the coil side of the ignition wires, the intake plenum has to be removed.

When I was shopping for ignition leads, I first looked at the stock replacement wires, because these were designed for Rover vehicles. Normally, I would just tell you to go with these, but they are typically $30.00 per wire and for a much lower price you can have a bit more performance and longevity. My two recommendations are the performance set from STI, which is what I have used with no problems, or the hands down best wires are from Magnacore. Magnacore wires are a solid core wire, which reduce the amount of resistance to less than 100 Ohms per foot and are melt proof. These will typically last the life of the vehicle.

Magnacore wires are not available at most auto parts stores but can be ordered from Atlantic British.

Rear Gate Handle

I know this sounds weird but Rover rear gate handles sit inside an air scoop at the back of the vehicle, getting soaked with dust and road grime. After a while, the handle will stop returning to the closed position and disallow the rear gate from staying closed.

Fortunately, Land Rover installed a removable emblem at the rear handle which allows for easy access to the assembly. All that needs to be done is pop the emblem off with a small screw driver. The handle mechanism will need to be cleaned really well to start. I will usually pop off the emblem just before going to the car wash. Once clean and dry, just spray some WD-40 or a comparable lubricant into the hole and pop the emblem back in. If it is really stuck, you might need to work the handle back and forth until it loosens up.

 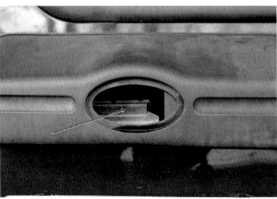

Windshield Wipers

When the windshield wipers go bad on a Discovery II owners will find it very difficult to find replacements. Land Rover found it necessary to use windshield wipers exclusive to this vehicle, they can be found in very few places and at a premium price.

Thankfully, windshield wiper arms from the Discovery I can be used. These accept standard 18 inch refills that can be picked up anywhere; the only drawback is that they do not look as nice.

One option is to pick them up used at a junk yard off an old Discovery I. Atlantic British has a kit that comes with everything needed and for almost the same price as the replacement stock wipers. Another benefit is the Discovery I wiper arms have more down pressure on the wiper blades for added performance in heavy rain.

Atlantic British sells a Discovery 1 windshield wiper conversion kit.

Maintenance Schedule

This is the maintenance schedule I use and recommend for almost any vehicle:

At Every Fueling

- Check engine oil level
- Use an upper cylinder lubricant/fuel system cleaner such as Marvel Mystery Oil or Lucas. This is not a must but it is the best way to keep the top half of the engine clean and lubricated. I have actually had better mileage with the Lucas.

Every 5,000 miles:

- Change the engine oil and replace the oil filter
- Grease all of the Zirk fittings
- Check all hoses for swelling and cracking. Lightly pull on each hose to make sure it is secure.
- Check belt(s) for cracking or fraying
- Check the air filter (see if light still shines through it).
- Clean the Mass Airflow Meter with CRC cleaner
- Do a visual inspection of the other fluids and top off. DO NOT top off the brake fluid unless it is very low! Then find out where it is going!

- Check for any fluid leaks
- Rotate the tires
- Check and set the tire pressure
- Top off the windshield washer Solvent

Every 15,000 Miles:

In addition to the 5,000 mile service:

- Lubricate locks and hinges on all doors
- Check brakes for wear and any other problems
- Check the steering components for play
- Check the shock absorbers for seepage

Every 30,000 Miles:

In addition to the 5,000 and 15,000 mile service:

- Replace the engine coolant; unless using a long service coolant
- Perform a transmission service or flush
- Replace the brake fluid
- Perform a fuel induction cleaning
- Get an alignment
- Clean the battery terminals
- Change the transfer case oil
- If not using a upper cylinder lubricant at re-fueling, use BG 44k here.

Every 60,000 Miles:

In addition to the rest:

- Replace spark plugs
- Replace ignition cables; unless using Magnacore
- Replace front and rear differential fluid
- Replace the power steering fluid

Recommended Maintenance Products

I have included my recommendations for products in each section throughout this book. I put them here again for easy reference:

Oil

My favorite oil is from Valvoline. Every mechanic I have known recommends Valvoline or at least respects it. The Rover V8 uses a flat tappet camshaft and will benefit from extra ZDDP so I recommend MaxLife.

Valvoline MaxLife 5W30

Oil Filter

For oil filter I use the Fram Ultra Synthetic. I never was a fan of Fram in the past but this filter is extremely well made, widely available and inexpensive.

Fram Ultra Synthetic

Differential and Transfer Case Fluid

Mobil 1 produces one of the best gear lubricants on the market and can actually free up some power. Some of the other gear oils on the market can foam up or simply fail under hard use, even the really expensive ones.

Mobil 1 75w90 Full Synthetic

Transmission Fluid

Again, I use Valvoline MaxLife ATF in automatic Transmission. This stuff simply rocks and is the favorite of many repair shops.

Valvoline MaxLife ATF

Power Steering Fluid

Land Rovers like synthetic power steering fluid. This stuff is amazing, it flows at -76° F and will not catch fire until it reaches 455°. The best, in my opinion, is Pentosin CHF 11s. If this is not available, just make sure it is synthetic.

Pentosin CHF 11s

Coolant

Coolant today is all pretty good. For simplicity reasons and compatibility, I recommend any Hybrid-OAT brand, the (yellow) universal stuff. Also, if taking it to a repair shop, the recycled stuff is very good. If your vehicle still has the orange, DEX Cool "OAT" coolant, DO NOT add anything but this to the cooling system. Even some of the universal coolants will have a bad reaction with the orange stuff.

Brake Fluid

Brake fluid has to meet certain safety parameters so any DOT 4 or 5.1 brands will work. Do not use DOT 5.

DOT 4 or DOT 5.1

Spark Plugs

Rover V8s are fine with almost any spark plug that will fit. I have had really good luck with the Denso PK16TT Platinum TT plugs.

Denso PK16TT Platinum TT

Ignition Cables

The best ignition cables available are the set from Magnecore, they will pretty much last forever and deliver a better spark.

Magnacore

Other Problems Upgrades and Repairs

This section is designed to cover anything that was not covered previously and for those who do not want their Rover looking like the next guys.

Plastic Rocker Panels

The stock Discovery rocker panels are made from molded ABS plastic. These rocker panels look nice and will not rust, but they will not protect the vehicle. The first time the Rover high centers on a rock or any other hard surface, the door is unlikely to open again.

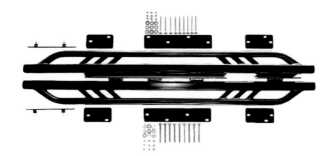

Many companies provide replacement, heavy-gauge steel rocker guards with jacking points. Jacking points come in very handy if you get stuck. These are also sometimes called rock sliders and will keep the Rover from getting un-repairable body damage when in the rough. These will also make vehicles look subtlety cooler and tougher. The best ones I have found are from Rocky Road Outfitters. They offer more protection and are at a better price than the competition.

Winch and Winch Bumpers

The Discovery's front bumper is functional and looks nice but the plastic has a tendency to crack easily with minor collisions. Many after market companies as well as the dealer sell replacement pieces but, for the same price a full steel welded unit can be had. I do strongly recommend one of these for any kind of trail use but they do have a drawback; mainly weight. Most are about 100lbs heavier than the original and will require heavy duty springs to be installed in the front. Also when a winch is added to the bumper another 60 to 80lbs is also added. Even with the heavy duty springs, you will feel the girth up front with added sway in corners and diving under hard braking.

Terrafirma Bumper and Skid Plate

The first bonus to a heavy steel bumper with a winch is, of course, looks. Secondly, while off road you can push over small trees, bounce the front off of rocks and handle steeper approach angles with almost no damage. Finally, there is nothing better than a winch when stuck. As long as there is a tree, a boulder or another vehicle you can get your Rover back out.

Two of the most popular steel bumpers are made by ARB and Terra Firma. The ARB is very cool looking and almost indestructible but the heavier of the two. When shopping for an aftermarket bumper, just make sure it will cover the huge windshield washer reservoir that is mounted at the front of the vehicle. Some off road bumpers will require this reservoir to be re-located.

Wheel Arches

Land Rover wheel arches do not hold up well to the elements. They fade, chalk and just really start to look bad. All other external black pieces will do the same. In contrast the paint and everything else holds up very well after many years which just make the arches look even worse. These ugly wheel arches can make an almost new Land Rover look old and neglected.

The first solution is to purchase a new set for roughly $400.00 from the factory and then install them. There is also another solution, if larger tires are installed. MM4x4 sells a 2 inch wider, pocket style aftermarket set for around $250.00. These are made of fade resistant, unbreakable ABS plastic and would be a good option for that off-road look.

Another option, and the one I used, is to refinish them. This takes about the same amount of time as installing new ones and at a fraction of the price.

1. Choose a product you would like to use. I chose a rubberized coating from Rust-oleum called Flexidip because of its incredible durability. Another brand and one better known is Plastidip. This stuff is great, easy to use, and will hold up to anything. Some people even paint their whole vehicle with this stuff and keep it on for years without issue. This procedure can also be used on all of the other black plastic parts that no longer look so good such as the grill, bumpers, and side trim. Another project this coating is ideal for is to re-paint and color-match the vehicles wheels. If you get tired of the color it will   peel off without hassle.

2. Sand and clean the wheel arches. Use a medium to fine grit sand paper to smooth down all of the rough patches but be careful not to scratch the paint. Next, very thoroughly clean each wheel arch with oil and wax removing solvent such as Clean-Strip Prep All. This will get any wax or plastic treatment out of all the nooks and crannies and assure good product adhesion.

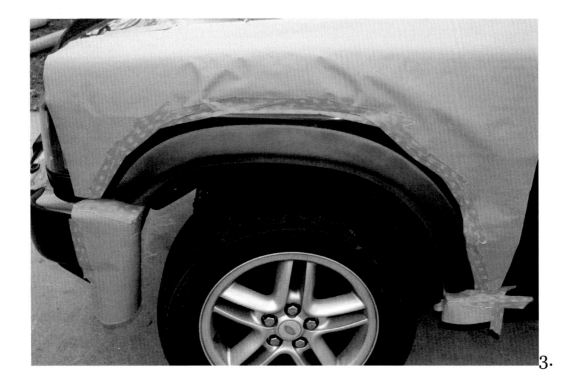

3.

Mask off around the wheel arches. Leave about a 2 inch gap between the masking edge and the wheel arch. I know this seems weird but keep reading.

4. Coat the wheel arches. With this type of coating get as much

of the product on the vehicles paint as on the wheel arches. Apply in four even coats making the last a heavy coat. This final heavy coat will smooth the surface and fill in any imperfections. DO NOT apply so heavy that the coating drips.

5. Peel off the overspray. Once dry, carefully remove the masking from the vehicle. Be careful not to prematurely peel off the coating from the paint. With the masking removed, pick at one of the edges of the coating with a finger nail or a toothpick. Now simply peel off all of the excess coating. This will leave a perfect line all the way around the wheel arch. If you accidentally over sprayed on to an unintended area, a micro fiber towel will clean it right off, with a bit of scrubbing.

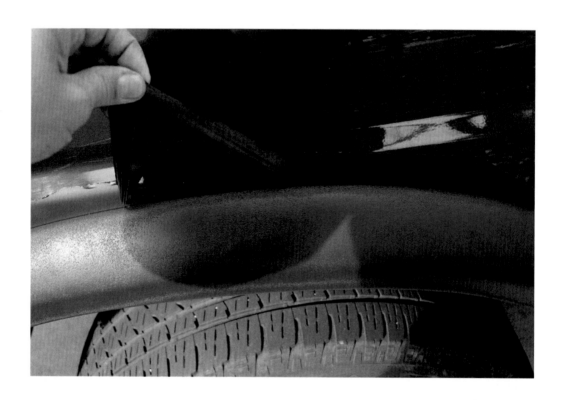

Fuel Door Latch

The only thing that holds the fuel filler door closed on a Discovery is a cheap piece of plastic. Unfortunately, these break if the clip is not aligned when the door is closed. Fortunately, they are available at Atlantic British for super cheap and I always keep a spare in the glove box. They are easy to install and need no tools, just be careful not to break it during installation.

Fuel Door Latch

Crankshaft Sensor Issues

Issues that the crankshaft sensor can cause are usually the most misdiagnosed. The crankshaft sensor is the only sensor without a backup and will leave a Land Rover stranded if it fails completely. Typically when this sensor starts to go bad the vehicle will have infuriating, nearly impossible to figure out gremlins. Some of these can be: hard starting when hot, multiple misfires when cold or the vehicle simply stops running and then will start right back up again when it cools down. How are you supposed to figure that out? I have seen mechanics throw every part, that might be the culprit, at a Land Rover then proceed to pull all of their hair out. This sensor is a bit of a pain to replace but if the above symptoms are occurring it is better than throwing money at it.

Poor Fuel Economy

Poor fuel economy and the words Land Rover are synonymous, at least here in the United States where we can not get a diesel. Typically, most V8 Rovers get roughly 13 to 15 miles to the gallon. A Rover in an un-maintained state can see as low as 9 to 12 MPG. There are no magic devices or pills that can make a big difference in economy that I know of and I have tried a few. Here are a few effective ways to raise your MPGs.

The first consideration is driving habits. Good driving habits can gain up to 15% in fuel savings. Most people have run across these suggestions somewhere in their driving careers, especially when fuel prices rise. Here are some of the more effective things to consider:

Cold weather warm up

The Land Rover V8 has fairly loose tolerances and does need to warm up a bit in cold weather. In the old days we had to allow an engine to come up in temperature just to be driven due to being carbureted. With modern fuel injection a vehicle can be started and driven right away, even in the coldest weather. On a Land Rover allow only about one or two minutes of warm up. This should be enough to get the tolerances to tighten up and keep any parts from banging together. Excessive idling uses fuel without motion therefore lowering miles per gallon. Another drawback to all this idling is increased carbon build up in the combustion chambers.

Accelerate Smoothly

Smooth acceleration allows the sensors to keep the fuel ratio closer to ideal. Another benefit to a smooth take off is a more efficient conversion of a vehicles fuel to energy.

Travel Lightly

Every extra pound of weight in a vehicle uses extra fuel, especially up hills or accelerating. As a mechanic, I have had many instances where I had to empty 200 lbs of stuff out of a customer's trunk to access the rear strut tops. Also those struts probably would have lasted another 20,000 miles if not for all the extra weight.

Wind Resistance

Land Rovers are basically big boxes with wheels and have the aerodynamic efficiency of a brick. It is fairly easy to make this problem even worse. The addition of a big roof rack or a lift kit can severely increase wind resistance and reduce mileage.

Another factor to consider is highway speed. Most Land Rovers get their best fuel economy between 60 and 70 MPH on the highway. Just increasing cruising speed to 75 MPH can decrease economy by three MPG.

Drive Defensively

I find it infuriating to look in my rearview mirror and see someone following me so closely that I can see the color of their eyes. This is not only dangerous for both drivers but, the one doing the tailgating has to make constant speed adjustments which also kills fuel economy. Also, drafting does not work under 100 MPH so do not think you have a reason to tailgate like a race car driver. Driving like your hair is on fire, weaving in and out of traffic, again is dangerous and will suck a ton of gas. Plus, driving like a crazy person with no patience will just stress you out and every one in your car and everyone on the road with you. Finally, think of all of the fuel a traffic ticket or an insurance deductible will purchase. So sit back, relax and enjoy your Land Rover; you will get to your destination sooner or later and, a lot happier.

Maintenance

A healthy Land Rover will get much better fuel economy than an unhealthy one. Most think of dirty fuel injectors, dirty air filters and worn spark plugs as "maintenance" for good fuel economy; and they would be correct but, there is more. Old differential, transfer case fluid and engine oil can be even worse. As lubricants, even synthetics, age they thicken. This thickening causes fluidic drag which can put a big dent in the gas budget especially with a full time four wheel drive system.

Tires

Choosing the wrong tire for the environment a vehicle is driven in can also hurt fuel mileage. Here in Colorado, half of the trucks on the road have big mud tires and never see anything but pavement. The more aggressive a tire's tread the less easily it wants to roll and the more fuel it will take to keep said vehicle rolling. Another detractor to fuel mileage is to have too high of a load range. Tires achieve more load range by adding more plies and thus more weight. These heavier tires take much more fuel to get rolling and no Land Rover (short of military) will ever need anything more than a Standard Load (SL) rating. Finally, check the pressure in the tires monthly. Low pressure not only causes excessive wear it also causes more rolling resistance.

Tables and Specifications

V8 Engine Specifications

Type	90° V8
Bore	3.7 inches or 94 mm
Stroke 4.0	2.79 inches or 71.04mm
Stroke 4.6	3.22 inches or 81.92mm
Firing Order	1-8-4-3-6-5-7-2
Compression Ratio	9.35:1
Rotation	Clockwise from front
Horsepower 4.0	182 @ 4750 RPM
Horsepower 4.6	217 @ 4750 RPM
Maximum RPM	5000
Wet Weight With Accessories	402 lbs
Recommended Spark Plugs	Denso PK16TT
Spark Plug Gap	0.040 or 1mm
Idle Speed	660 RPM
Fuel Grade	Premium 91 to 93 RON
Oil Pressure @ Idle	10 PSI
Oil Pressure @ 2000 RPM	50 PSI

Cooling System

Type	Thermostatically controlled, pressurized water and antifreeze design with a vertical flow radiator. Pump assisted.
Fans	One 9 Blade belt driven with a viscous clutch and one 11 blade electric

Electric Fan On/Off Points With A/C On	On @ 212° F / 100° C Off @ 202° F / 94.4° C On @ less than 50 MPH and ambient temperature above 82° F / 27.7° C Off @ above 63 MPH or ambient temperature Below 77° F / 25° C
Coolant Pump	Belt driven from crankshaft, impeller type
Coolant Pump Output	2.64 Gallons @ 1000 RPM
Thermostat Type	Waxstat with pressure relief valve
Thermostat Fully Open Stock	204° F / 95.5° C
Recommended Warm Weather Thermostat Fully Open	190° / 87.7° C
Expansion Tank Cap Relief pressure	20 PSI

Automatic Transmission

Type	ZF4HP22, electric/hydraulic with lock up torque converter
Gears	4 forward & 1 Reverse
Ratios: First Second Third Fourth Reverse	 2.480:1 1.480:1 1.00:1 0.728:1 2.086:1
Torque Converter Lock Up	Third or fourth gear above 45 MPH

Manual Transmission

Type	R380 Constant Mesh
Gears	5 Forward, 1 Reverse all synchromesh
First	3.321:1
Second	2.132:1
Third	1.397:1
Fourth	1.00:1
Fifth	0.732:1
Reverse	3.536:1
Clutch Type	Diaphragm spring, hydraulically operated with preloaded release bearing.

Transfer Case

Type	LT230SE 2 Speed Reduction
Reduction Ratio	1.211:1 High Range 3.32:1 Low Range
Drive	Front & rear split lockable differential

Front and Rear Axles

Front Axle Type	Solid axle casing with drive shafts and constant velocity joints
Rear Axle Type	Solid axle casing with drive shafts
Gear Reduction Ratio	3.538:1

Steering

Type	Hydraulically assisted worm & roller
Steering Wheel Turns Lock to	3.5

Lock	
Steering Wheel Diameter	15.7 inches or 400mm
Turning Circle	39.1 Feet or 11.9 metres
Power Steering Pump	Hobourn Series 500, belt driven
Power Steering Pump Pressure	305 PSI @ idle / 900 PSI @ full lock

Suspension

Front Type	Beam axle with coil springs, longitudinal radius arms and panhard rod. Twin tube or mono tube shock absorbers with an anti roll bar or active cornering enhancement (ACE)
Nominal Height From Hub Center to Wheel Arch	19.7 inches or 500mm
Bump Stop Height	1.75 inches or 44.5mm
Anti Roll Bar Diameter With ACE	1.38 inches or 35mm
Anti Roll Bar Diameter Without ACE	1.18 inches or 30mm
Rear Type	Beam type with coil or air springs, longitudinal radius arms and a Watts linkage. Twin tube or mono tube shock absorbers with an anti roll bar or active cornering enhancement.
Nominal Height From Hub Center to Wheel Arch	Coil Spring 19.0 inches or 483mm Air Spring 18.6 inches or 473mm
Bump Stop Height	Coil Spring 2.8 inches or 71.5mm

	Air Spring 2.4 inches or 61.5mm
Anti Roll Bar Diameter	1.38 inches or 35mm With ACE 1.14 inches or 29mm With Air Springs .75 inches or 19mm With Coil Springs

Brakes

Type	Vacuum assisted, diagonally split hydraulic disc with four channel Antilock
Disc Diameter	Front 11.693 inches or 297mm Rear 11.961 inches or 303.8mm
Minimum Disc Thickness	Front 0.980 inches or 25mm New Maximum Limit 0.866 inches or 22mm Rear 0.492 inches or 12.5mm New Maximum Limit 0.461 inches or 11.7mm
Minimum Pad Thickness	0.079 inches or 2.0mm
Parking Brake	Cable operated drum on the transfer case rear output shaft.

Dimensions

Overall Length	186.6 inches or 4715mm
Overall Width	74.2 inches or 1885mm
Overall Height	76.4 inches or 1940mm
Minimum Ground Clearance	10 inches or 253.5mm

Wheelbase	100 inches or 2540mm
Track Front	60.63 inches or 1540mm
Track Rear	61.42 inches or 1560mm

Weights

Unloaded Weight	4619-4928 lbs or 2095-2235 kgs
Maximum Gross Vehicle Weight	Coil spring 6063 lbs / 2750 kgs Air Spring 6228 lbs / 2825 kgs
Maximum Front Axle Load	2646 lbs or 1200 kgs
Maximum Rear Axle Load	Coil Springs 3792 lbs or 1720 kgs Air Springs 3968 lbs or 3968 kgs

Capacities

Fuel Tank	25.5 gal	95 liters
Engine Oil Change With Filter with oil cooler without oil cooler	 6.6 qts 6.1 qts	 6.27 liters 6.27 liters
Automatic Transmission From Dry	9.85 qts	9.7 liters
Manual Transmission Refill With Cooler	3.0 qts	2.8 liters
Manual Transmission Refill Without Cooler	2.4 qts	2.3 liters
Transfer Case Refill	2.05 qts	2.0 liters
Front & Rear Axle Refill	1.7 qts	1.6 liters
Cooling System Refill	3.1 gal	12 liters

Notes

Made in the USA
Columbia, SC
24 March 2019